**KOREA TOWARDS
ANTI-AMERICA**

Copyright © 2019 by Se-eui Kim

All rights reserved

Garosero Yeonguso, B1 Apgujeong-ro 12gil 42, Gangnam-gu, Seoul, Republic of Korea

For information about permission to reproduce selections from this book, send an e-mail to hoverlab2018@gmail.com

First published 2019

Book design by Design camp
Printed in the Republic of Korea

ISBN : 979-11-966619-0-8 03340

KOREA TOWARDS ANTI-AMERICA

Se-eui Kim

CONTENTS

Background of the Author (About the Author)   006

0. Prologue
0-1. The Republic of Korea Sharply Divided by the Left Wing and the Right Wing   014

1. Why Anti-Americanism?
1-1. Why Anti-Americanism?   024
1-2. North Korean Infiltration of the Republic of Korea   026
1-3. Leftist Forces' Infiltration of the South Korean Armed Forces   028
1-4. Why is Anti-Japan Just As Important to the Left as Anti-America   031
1-5. Moon Jae-in Administration's Attempt to Erase the Rhee Syng-man Administration   040

2. Korea's Core Anti-American Group, the "386 Generation"
2-1. Anti-American Movement Started in Gwangju   046
2-2. 1987 June Uprising and NL   048
2-3. An Incident That Showed How Terrifying NL Really Is   058

3. Notable Examples of Anti-American Movement
3-1. Terrorism attack Against the Official Residence of the US Ambassador to Korea   064
3-2. President-elect Kim Dae-jung and the Full-fledged Movement of 386 Generation   066
3-3. No Gun Ri Incident, US Troops in Korea, and the Movie 'Host'   068
3-4. Apolo Anton Ohno and the Anti-American Movement   070
3-5. The Worst Traffic Accident and Candlelight Rallies   072
3-6. Callous to the Battle of Yeonpyeong? Political Motivation Controversy   077
3-7. Protest Against U.S. Beef   082
3-8. Knife Attack on U.S. Ambassador to Korea Mark Lippert   090

4. Current Situation of Anti-American Activists in the Moon Jae-in Administration
4-1. National Council of Student Representatives — What Do They Do?   094
4-2. Politicians from the National Council of Student Representatives (NL)   096
4-3. Politicians from Non-NCSR Organizations (PD)   104
4-4. Minbyun, a Lawyers' Society Aligning Itself with Left-wing Government   107

5. Current Status of the Korean Media

5-1. The Birth of the National Union of Media Workers (NUM)	112
5-2. One of the Most Radical Union's Strike in MBC	123
5-3. The Bias of the National Union of Media Workers (NUM)	127
5-4. Structure of the National Union of Media Workers	135
5-5. Naver, a Left-leaning Portal	138
5-6. Druking Scandal Exposes the Manipulation of Public Opinion	141
5-7. A Significant Incident That Made Naver Stop Editing News Stories	148
5-8. Naver Labor Union Joins National Council of Trade Unions	153
5-9. Presidential Chief Secretary and MBC Chief Editor with a Daum Background / DAUM	154
5-10. Appointment of KBS and MBC Presidents and the National Union of Media Workers	156
5-11. Democratic Party of Korea Attempts to Occupy the Broadcasting Industry	163
5-12. Secret Inspection and Retaliation in MBC	165

6. Examples of the Korean Press Seized by the Korea Confederation of Trade Unions

6-1. Overestimated Candlelight Rallies, Underestimated Taegukgi Rallies	174
6-2. Abolishment of the Rule about Estimates Both by the Organizers and the Police	180
6-3. The Press Pulls Even the US Embassy in Seoul into the Candlelight Rally	184
6-4. Human Rights issues in North Korea being Ignored by the South Korean Press	187
6-5. Overextended Praise of Kim Jong-un	193
6-6. North Korea Praise in Full Swing Beginning with the Pyongchang Olympics	196
6-7. Ludicrous Fascination with Kim Yo-jong	198
6-8. The Press Becomes the Spokespersons for the North about the Cheonan Sinking Incident	203
6-9. The Press Accuses Fishermen of responsibility for the Second Battle of Yeonpyeong	213
6-10. JTBC Plays a Leading Role in Inciting Issues Regarding the US THAAD Deployment	219
6-11. The Korean Press Siding with the North Blaming the United States	233
6-12. MBC is Uncomfortable with the Expression of "The North is Our Enemy"	236
6-13. The Korean Press Accuses the US Vice President Mike Pence for Being Rude	239

7. Moving Forward to the Era of New Media

7-1. Trump Declares War on Fake News	244
7-2. The Need for a Counter Labor Union	247
7-3. The Status of Alternative Journalism in Korea	251
7-4. Moving Beyond the Conservative vs. Liberal Frame	256

8. Epilogue   264

9. Works Cited   270

Koreans regard humility as a virtue. And when offered a favor, Koreans refuse to accept it at least once. They believe that's a gesture of courtesy. Sometimes that gesture is misunderstood. Of course, it is slightly different now that Korean society has adopted Western customs and conduct. But Koreans are still not inclined to self-promotion.

I can claim to have gone through more than most other reporters. First, I was once sentenced to a year in prison by the court. It was a severe punishment, but a very interesting experience. Of course, I was bitter at the time of sentencing. It all started when I made an accusatory report about the Joint Armed Forces Headquarters located in Gyeryong-si, South Chungcheong Province on February 6, 2007. The Joint Armed Forces Headquarters is the de facto heart of the ROK armed forces where the Chief of Staff of the ROK Army, Navy and Air Force has his office. It can be compared to the Pentagon of America, except that the building is an octagon instead of a pentagon. In American terms, it could be called the Octagon. If the Ministry of National Defense in Yongsan-gu, Seoul is the administrative center of the military where the Minister of Defense has his office, the Joint Armed Forces Headquarters in Gyeryong-si, South Chungcheong Province is the center of military operations.

It turned out that a hostess bar had been doing business in this important military facility that required the highest security. That's what I exposed in my MBC exclusive report. The report had such an impact that follow-up coverage had to be aired the next day. I was able to cover the story because I had served in that very headquarters. While in service, I was an Air Force staff sergeant in charge of communication, and some of my peers worked as waiters in the hostess bar that was running on the base in Gyeryong. I was shocked that a hostess bar was operating in the heart of the ROK armed forces and civilian hostesses were drinking and singing with soldiers, and more than anything, I found it abhorrent that soldiers were pulled out to work as waiters at the hostess bar instead of serving and defending the country as they were supposed to. It was outrageous. So I was determined to expose the issue when I become a journalist someday, and I was acting on that aim when I made the report. When it broke, the Roh Moo-hyun administration assumed a firm stand. But the firm stand was not against the military. Rather, his administration targeted the journalist who'd exposed it. I was immediately indicted for having trespassed on a military base and leaking a military secret. During the trial that followed, they seemed to have dropped the trespassing charge perhaps because it was an embarrassment even by their standards. Eventually, I was sentenced to one year in prison with a stay of execution for two years by the military court on April 24, 2008. Journalists groups including the Journalists Association of Korea, the Korean Broadcast Journalist Association and the MBC Reporters' Union immediately issued statements in protest against the decision, and many online users joined in the campaign to appeal the judgement. After a long court battle that ensued, the Supreme Court made the final decision on January 30, 2009 in which I was sentenced to one year in prison with suspension of the sentence for two years. It naturally makes me wonder how many reporters in Korea were ever convicted and handed one year in jail in blatant retaliation for what they had reported. None to that date, I believe.

Secondly, I am one of the very few reporters who'd been to Pyongyang, North Korea, for news coverage. It was on October 12, 2005 that I departed Shenyang, China, and flew to Pyongyang on an airplane that belonged to Air Koryo, the state-owned national flag carrier airline of North Korea. The three-nights-four-days visit to Pyongyang was a priceless experience to me. There were a few reporters who visited Kaesong Industrial Complex or Mt. Keumgang to cover stories about the reunion of war-separated families, but it was extremely rare for a reporter from the South to go to Pyongyang in the North for general news coverage. Being under the Roh Moo-hyun administration, the visit was possible because Kim Jong-il was bringing in people from the South in time for a mass gymnastics and arts event called the Arirang Festival. There were some South Koreans who paid several thousands of dollars to the North to get permission to visit the North as well.

Pyongyang is an extremely isolated, closed society, but unlike the majority of North Koreans, the residents of Pyongyang were a privileged class. Even so, the lifestyle of the Pyongyang residents was so poor that it could not compare to the living conditions of South Koreans. I even witnessed rogue government employees taking bribes like those in typical third world countries. A few North Koreans who belonged to the North's State Security Agency were in charge of keeping an eye on our reporting crew, and they followed us everywhere to monitor us while we covered stories about Pyongyang. The State Security Agency is similar to the National Security Planning Agency of the South. During our tour in Pyongyang, our reporting crew was able to secretly interview a few Pyongyang citizens, and to our surprise, they were not even aware that South Koreans were visiting to watch the Arirang Festival. It spoke volumes about what an isolated society it really was. The North's security agents tried to make issues out of this, but we were able to get away with it by bribing them with about 500 euros. Those were really significant interviews, but the MBC newsroom decided not to air them perhaps because they might damage the South-North relationship.

Third, I'm a founder of a labor union. On March 6, 2013, I established a labor union in MBC. Up until then, MBC had no unions other than the National Union of Media Workers that is under the umbrella of the Korean Confederation of Trade Unions. I was hired by MBC in December 2004 and was sent to a training institute where the leaders of the National Union of Media Workers introduced the union to us and encouraged us to join. By the time the training was over, practically every trainee had joined the National Union of Media Workers. I will discuss in further detail later, but I've experienced numerous strikes while working for MBC, but none of the strikes were about demanding better benefits for the union members. All those strikes were about political issues. One of the most remarkable strikes was the one that took place in 2012 and lasted for a whopping 170 days at the painful cost of union members who had to join the strike to support the handful of union leaders' politically charged cause. During the entire 170-day strike — which was close to six months — over 1,000 striking union members struggled because they were not paid a single penny by the company. I thought nobody in the Korean news media should be forced to become a scapegoat to satisfy such a collectivistic uniformity. That's why I decided to form a labor union despite criticism from the National Union of Media Workers. At the time, I was just an ordinary reporter, and not even on a manager level. That meant I was putting myself up for an unthinkable challenge, considering how the Korean news media world was run by the rule of seniority. So I asked senior reporters to be the head of the labor union I was going to form. But the senior reporters said they would join the union, but none of them agreed to serve as the union boss. I had no choice but to establish a labor union and become the head of it myself. I was sincerely willing to carry the cross on my shoulder. I was unable to find a senior reporter who was willing to chair the union, and in the end, I ended up serving as the union head for four and a half years. It was a great experience.

And I am a little embarrassed to do this, but I want to disclose one more fact because of its significance as a record. According to a Joongang Daily report dated January 28, 2018, Kim Se-eui ranked number one among the celebrities most favored by voters who supported the Liberal Korean Party's presidential candidate Hong Jun-pyo in the 2017 presidential election. The Vancouver Olympic gold medalist Kim Yuna ranked second, following after Kim Se-eui. The third most favorite celebrity was Hyemin Sunim, the fourth was JTBC President Sohn Suk-hee, and the fifth was Bill Gates. A research team led by Professor Lee Won-jae of KAIST Graduate School of Culture Technology — a school known to attract Korea's most brilliant science and engineering students — analyzed the political orientations of Facebook users through social network analysis techniques. According to the results, while there was no

BACKGROUND OF THE AUTHOR (ABOUT THE AUTHOR)

big difference in preference of politicians and celebrities among Moon Jae-in, Ahn Cheol-su, Yoo Seung-min and Shim Sang-jung supporters, there was a noticeable difference among the Hong Jun-pyo supporters. In particular, the "celebrities" category turned up a rather surprising result because I ranked number one even though I was just a reporter whose popularity could not be even compared to such famous celebrities as Kim Yuna, Sohn Suk-hee, and Bill Gates. When the analysis results were announced, Joongang Daily kindly added "Kim Se-eui is an MBC reporter" to explain who I was. Kim Se-eui may not be a widely recognized name, but the analysis results showed how a new celebrity can be born in a new media channel such as Facebook, or among people with specific political preferences. Right now, the global media environment is going through a rapid change in Korea as well as in the world. We have to realize how a lesser-known figure can quickly emerge as a new star through the changing media environment such as social media, and how a new media can unleash significant influence. That is exactly what motivated me to write this book.

0. PROLOGUE

0-1.
THE REPUBLIC OF KOREA SHARPLY DIVIDED BY THE LEFT WING AND THE RIGHT WING

The Republic of Korea has never been so polarized between left and right. Civil movements that pulled people out of their houses to rally starting in the 1980s and running up until 2016 were largely attributed to the leftists. But after the 2016 protest that came to be known as the "Candlelight Rally" and the following conservatives' protest that came to be known as "Taegukgi Rally", both leftists and rightists are turning out on streets to rally.

Some people may not be sure if the Right can take as much credit as the Left. Perhaps they heard a lot about candlelight rallies, but little about Taegukgi rallies. Could it be that they heard little about Taegukgi rallies because the scale was far less than the candlelight rallies?

No, absolutely not. People heard little about them because major Korean news media channels did not bother to cover stories about Taegukgi rallies. So the question is: Why did major Korean news media channels pay less attention to Taegukgi rallies than they did to candle rallies?

There are many theories, but I will explain one of them in detail later on.

0. PROLOGUE

Candlelight Rallies and Taegukgi Rallies.

Now, let me talk about the protests by the rightists, who started taking to the street like the leftists had been doing and have been rallying more passionately and persistently than the leftists.

The so-called Taegukgi rally, which became synonymous with protests by conservative right-wing ideologists, is worth a study.

Upon close examination, you will find something very interesting with the protests rallied by the Right.

As the term indicates, the conservatives' protests came to be known as Taegukgi rallies because they carry the Korean national flag as the main symbol. However, there is another national flag that never fails to accompany Taegukgi in their rallies: The Stars and Stripes.

One might wonder: What does the American national flag have to do with their demonstrations?

Does that mean other national flags such as the Union Jack of the United Kingdom or the Tricolour of France might appear in their rallies as well?

How about the flag of the United Nations whose forces provided us

A large US flag that appeared in the Taegukgi rallies.

with critical help during the Korean War?

Then, beginning in 2018, another national flag started playing an important role in the Taegukgi rallies along with the American Stars and Stripes: the flag of Israel, marked by the iconic Star of David.

Israel established diplomatic relations with Korea in 1962, but the Korea-Israel relations suffered a little setback during the 1970s when Korean construction companies became major developers in the Middle Eastern regions.

Israel didn't send their forces to support us during the Korean War either. Given that, I assume that the flag of Israel started to make its appearance in their demonstrations as the Korean conservative protesters' gesture to show what they have in mind to the US government including US President Donald Trump.

President Trump made an official acknowledgement of Jerusalem as the capital of Israel despite criticism from the international community. Then shortly after, the flag of Israel appeared in Korean conservatives' protests out of the blue along with the flag of the United States. We need to examine this development as well.

0. PROLOGUE

An Israeli flag that appeared in the Taegukgi rallies.

Understandably, there are people who criticize this phenomenon. They wonder why the Stars and Stripes has to show up in rallies about issues that concern the Republic of Korea. Some of them also criticize turning to a foreign country for support.

I myself stand negative on this issue as well, because I cannot understand why they have to bring in a national flag of another country for an issue we have to resolve on our own. But it is still worth careful consideration because it clearly shows how much the United States means to the Korean right-wing activists. Which begs the question: Why do the Korean rightists put so much significance to our relations with the United States? The answer can be found more easily if you think about this question from an opposite perspective and ask: Why are the leftists are so geared towards anti-Americanism?

There is something we need to address before we find out why anti-Americanism is so prevalent among Korean leftists. One of the reasons is that Korea was able to become a liberal democratic and capitalistic country instead of turning into a socialist state like North Korea did all because Korea had help from numerous allies including the United States.

Korean War veterans memorial in Washington D.C.

The United States, in particular, was willing to sacrifice many precious American lives to keep the Republic of Korea from turning into a communist state. In Washington DC, US, there is the Korean War Veterans Memorial. Most Koreans only visit the Lincoln Memorial that stands behind the Korean War Veterans Memorial as tourist groups and take keepsake photos there. But I believe that Koreans must to go to the Korean War Veterans Memorial and express appreciation for their sacrifices. There is a touching sentence inscribed on a granite wall as well: Freedom is not free.

It is a truly powerful message. Korea was able to grow to be what it is today all thanks to the many American soldiers who sacrificed their youth and even their lives to protect the freedom of a small Asian country.

In the Korean War, 36,516 U.S. soldiers lost their lives, another 103,248 were wounded, and 8,177 were missing in action. Also, young soldiers from the United Kingdom, Canada, Australia, Turkey, France, and many other countries also sacrificed their precious lives in the Korean

0. PROLOGUE

War. Including the American servicemen, the total casualties of the UN allied forces are estimated to be 58,000 fatalities and over 150,000 injuries.

The Republic of Korea was able to become what it is today all thanks to the efforts and sacrifices of the United States and the UN allied forces. This should never be forgotten.

The anti-Americanists refuse to acknowledge their sacrifices. They claim that numerous lives were sacrificed to satisfy the interests of the US government. However, that is not true.

The presence of our powerful ally, the United States, takes a significant part in ensuring the security of Korea considering the special circumstances of the Korean Peninsula that is divided into North and South and under constant military tension.

Ironic as it is, however, Korea has just as many, if not more, anti-Americanists as any country in the world. Worse, they are not just a marginalized group in our society: they account for a significant portion of the leadership of Korean politics. One can only wonder how on earth these anti-American groups of people could have grown to take over the mainstream of the Korean society.

First, let's take a look at the few examples that show how prevalent the anti-American sentiment is in Korea.

Korea's leading daily newspaper Chosun Ilbo printed an article on April 5, 2008 that shocked a lot of readers. The article was about the results of a survey conducted by Kim Choong-bae, the former principal of Korean Military Academy, in January 2004 and answered by 250 students who were admitted to the Korean Military Academy. The students were asked, "Who is our primary enemy?" Most Koreans have been

Anti-American protesters

taught "our primary enemy is North Korea" for decades. However, a 34% of the students answered it was "the United States," and 33% of them answered it was North Korea. According to the result, the United States was our primary enemy and North Korea was only a secondary enemy in the minds of the students. The Korean Military Academy is literally the incubator of Korea's military officers, who will then play an essential role in our military as elite ROK army officers. That made the result all the more shocking.

In the same year, 2004, the Ministry of Defense carried out a consciousness survey of soldiers who had just started their service. The results showed that as much as 75% of them were leaning towards anti-Americanism. Only 36% of the respondents answered that liberal democracy was better than communism.

How do we explain these results? We can find the answer rather easily by looking at the administrations of the early 2000s, their political orientation, and events that followed. Some might wonder why I bring up the past at a time when we are headed toward 2020.

But we must remember how Korea was under the power of left-leaning administrations during the administrations of President Kim Dae-jung and Roh Moo-hyun from 1998 to 2008. For the following nine years beginning with the Lee Myung-bak administration to the time President Park Geun-hye was impeached and left office, the power was in the hands of right-wing administrations. Since the left-wing administration led by President Moon Jae-in took office in 2017, the previous left-wing ideologists were able to return and continue their lineage till the present time.

So let's go back to how anti-American sentiment became prevalent in the Republic of Korea.

1. WHY ANTI-AMERICANISM?

1-1.
WHY ANTI-AMERICANISM?

Anti-Americanism flourished the most in the early 2000s under the left-wing administrations of President Kim Dae-jung and Roh Moo-hyun. Before talking about anti-Americanism, we need to look at the history of those who have tried to proliferate anti-American sentiment for quite some time.

I have some reservations whenever I get onto this subject. There are people who may ask: Why still talk about the Korean War that happened in the 50s? In Korea, ideological orientation issue — often described in terms of "political colorism" in the Korean society — is as sensitive as the Political Correctness (PC) issue in America. There are a significant number of people who avoid talking about it, because they run the risk of being labeled as an extreme right or as someone falling behind the times just by bringing up the issue. Nevertheless, it must be addressed.

It happened not very long ago. On December 19, 2014, the ROK constitutional court delivered a final decision that effectively disbanded a political party. It was the day when the leftist United Progressive Party — which produced as many as 13 lawmakers, making it the third largest

1. WHY ANTI-AMERICANISM?

Disbandment of the Unified Progressive Party and the arrest of the lawmaker Lee Seok-ki.

party within the National Assembly — was disbanded on charges including plotting a rebellion, to everybody's shock. This will be explained in further details.

I am bringing up this story because I want to point out that, in Korea the ideological orientation — often described in terms of color, as in red for communism, in Korean society — is not just a matter of being extreme rightists, nor is it an antiquated debate chewed on by outdated old-timers. The Republic of Korea is still dealing with the dangerous regime of North Korea at close range. Now, the North Korean regime tries to act like they are earnestly wishing for a peaceful reunification just like it did during the Kim Dae-jung and Roh Moo-hyun administrations. But North Korea hasn't changed. The North Korean regime has always been targeting the Republic of Korea before and even after the Korean War, and there has been no change in their ultimate target.

1-2.
NORTH KOREAN INFILTRATION OF THE REPUBLIC OF KOREA

When do you think the Republic of Korea was born? It's after August 15, 1945 when Joseon was liberated from Japanese colonial rule. "Little Boy" — the code name of the nuclear bomb the United States dropped at Hiroshima, Japan, on August 6, 1945 — played a critical role for Joseon to achieve its independence from Japan.

However, the Korean Peninsula was divided at the 38th parallel by the United States and the Soviet Union during the process of disarming the Japanese forces, and subsequently began the ideological confrontation and intense espionage war between the two Koreas. It was from this point on that a significant number of North Korean forces secretly began taking action within South Korea.

Nam Jeong-wook, in his book, *Goodbye 386*, defined the Korean War as "a war where the North Korean military and South Korean leftists joined together". I agree. One of the characteristics of the Korean War was that it left so many civilian fatalities that were brutally killed. Interestingly enough, a majority of the civilian bodies were discovered in residential areas that were far from battlefields. And their MO was mostly execution style carried out by bamboo spear, sickle, and club instead of gunshot or bombing. As of June 28, 1950, South Korea had only 25,000 soldiers, but the number of leftists who were engaged in partisan activities at Mt. Jiri, which is located in the southernmost part of South Korea, is estimated to be at least 20,000 or even up to 60,000. That shows how meticulously North Korea had been preparing for the Korean War.

1-3.
LEFTIST FORCES' INFILTRATION OF THE SOUTH KOREAN ARMED FORCES

North Korea was threatening South Korea in a more frightening way. The US military government that took charge of South Korea after the nation's liberation from Japan selected South Korean soldiers only based on physical checkups and oral tests. Leftist forces under the command of the North Korean regime were able to infiltrate the South Korean armed forces rather easily because of the lack of more thorough background checks. If I may use this US incident as an example, in May 2016, a US Army 2nd Lt. named Spenser Rapone posted on Twitter a photo of himself wearing a Che Guevara shirt under his uniform at his West Point graduation along with the message "communism will win." Considering this happened in the United States as recently as 2016, one can only imagine how easy it would have been to mask their true identity and ideology in Korea during the 1940s.

Eventually, the leftist forces that infiltrated the South Korean armed forces instigated an incident that came to be known as the "Yeosu–Suncheon Rebellion" in March 1949. It turned out that the rebellion was led by 1,496 left-leaning soldiers — including 326 officers and 1,170 privates

1. WHY ANTI-AMERICANISM?

— and when the people who participated in it indirectly are included, the number of leftist rebels was a staggering 4,749. The South Korean government nabbed all these leftist rebels, and some of the more violent ones were executed in the process. On May 4, 1949, shortly after the rebellion, Kang Tae-moo and Pyo Moo-won — two army majors who were serving in the National Defense Guard — defected to North Korea along with hundreds of soldiers who belonged to their battalions. It meant a military force equal to two battalions were moved instantly from the South Korean armed forces to the North Korean military forces in a single, outrageous, daunting incident. In the case of Pyo Moo-won, he took 450 South Korean soldiers to the North and turned them into North Korean soldiers, and he was promoted to Lt. general in North Korea, while in the case of Kang Tae-moo, he turned 300 South Korean soldiers into North Korean soldiers and made it so far as becoming a Major General in the North Korean military.

On June 23, 1950, when North Korea's provocations and threats kept growing and expanding, the South Korean military made an absurd move to lift heightened security measures and granted furlough or outings to all military personnel. As a result, about one third of the South Korean military personnel were out of their barracks. We cannot pin blame only on incompetent commanders for this incident, because there is something very fishy about it: it happened at a time when the leftists forces under the command of North Korea were deeply infiltrating the South Korean armed forces. At 4:00 am on June 25, 1950, the Democratic People's Republic of Korea (DPRK) launched the offensive Operation Pokpoong (or Storm in English) against the Republic of Korea (ROK) and so began the Korean War. The North Korean forces numbered over 198,000 soldiers.

It turned out that the ROK Army Chief of Staff General Chae Pyong-dok was notified of this invasion belatedly because he was sleeping at the time. His aide-de-camp First Lt. Nah Choi-gwang was allegedly at the Chief of Staff's official residence when it happened. Upon being notified of the North's invasion of the South, Lt. Colonel Lim Boo-taek — who was in Chuncheon, Gangwon Province at the time — made an urgent call to General Chae Pyong-dok, but First Lt. Nah Choi-gwang told him that the General was sleeping and therefore could not come to the phone. Later on, Nah Choi-gwang went missing after the start of the Korean War, and his name was nowhere to be found in the list of South Korean army officers. There is good reason to question the true identity of this man named Nah Choi-gwang, who made that kind of a response in such a critical situation.

1-4.
WHY IS ANTI-JAPAN JUST AS IMPORTANT TO THE LEFT AS ANTI-AMERICA

Anti-Americanism is the easiest means by which the Left can attract people when spreading their complicated, multi-layered ideology. There is no easier way than using hatred to build a sense of identity with others by making someone a common enemy. According to Shim Yang-seop's book, *Anatomy of Anti-Americanism*, the ideology of the "386 generation" can be defined as "left nationalism." One example of left nationalist academics is Kang Man-gil, who included pro-Japanese ideologists in the same group as the pro-division and pro-cold war system ideologists. He also distinguishes the Left as pro-national liberation forces, and the Right, pro-division forces. According to him, the leftists are ultimately trying to promote the idea that the South and the North must reunite as one on the basis of being the same nation, and that the United States is the enemy to the Korean peninsula. In addition, the leftists often use anti-American and anti-Japanese sentiments to cast doubts about the legitimacy of the South Korean government. As we are all aware, North Korea was under the powerful influence of the USSR military rule while South Korea was under US military rule. The leftists believe that the US gave significant help to the right-leaning Korean government, and they hold resentment against the US because they think the US is interfering in South-North relations.

In addition, the leftists often take advantage of anti-Japanese sentiments so as to have people feel hatred against Japan, a country that can be of help in countering North Korea. In particular, the leftists use anti-Japanese sentiment to criticize Rhee Syng-man, the first and the last Head of State of the Provisional Government of the Republic of Korea, and to shatter the legitimacy of the South Korean government. On October 12, 1948, the ROK government created the Special Investigation Committee of Antinational Activists (SICAA). This was a committee created to purge pro-Japanese activists who had engaged in antinational activities during the 36 years of Japanese occupation. But during the process of identifying the pro-Japanese activists, the Republic of Korea experienced increasing internal conflicts. Concerned about the communist forces of the North expanding their influence into the South, the United States government wanted the South Korean government to be established and stabilized the soonest possible. That's the reason a significant number of pro-Japanese idealists were recruited by the US Military Government in Korea because

1. WHY ANTI-AMERICANISM?

Cho Seung-woo played as Kim Won-bong in the movie.

they had experience running a government during the 36 years of Japanese colonial rule. When President Rhee Syng-man took over the government after the end of the US military rule of Korea, his priority was also the stabilization of the government, and as the result, these pro-Japanese idealists ended up keeping their positions in various government agencies. For all these reasons, SICAA was unable to accomplish much before it wrapped up its activities. North Korea and the leftists, however, use it as an excuse to damage the government's legitimacy, claiming that "The ROK government failed to purge anti-Japanese activists." But North Korea is not in a position to claim that they did a better job when it comes to the anti-Japanese activist issue. For example, Kim Il-sung's younger brother Kim Young-ju was a pro-Japanese MP assistant during Japanese colonial days, yet, he was able to hold key posts in the North including Honorary Vice President of the Presidium of the Supreme People's Assembly.

The problem is that the anti-Japanese sentiment is also all too prevalent in South Korea as well. A significant number of blockbuster-level movies that are released each year are about fighting Japan. On July 22,

Lee Byung-hun (r.) played the role of Kim Won-bong (l.) in the movie.

2015, the movie "Assassin" was released in Korea. It was a big box-office hit with a ticket sales record pushing 12.7 million. However, the movie fueled anti-Japanese sentiment by depicting a North Korean figure — whose name had been a taboo in the South — as a heroic independence movement activist. That is the problem. The name of the figure was Kim Won-bong, — played by the actor Cho Seung-woo. In the movie, Kim Won-bong plays an impressive role in which he orchestrates all plans to purge pro-Japanese forces. In truth, Kim Won-bong was a communist to the bones, and he defected to the North where he served as vice chairman of the Standing Committee of the Supreme People's Assembly. According to the New Daily news article dated August 23, 2015, Kim Won-bong made it so far as Chairman of the National Censorship Committee, and there are records of his participation in the Korean War as well. In the past, he may have been an independent fighter who engaged in armed struggle for the independence of the Republic of Korea, but he was also a war criminal who'd pointed his gun at his fellow Koreans during the Korean War. However, those millions of Koreans who watched the block-

1. WHY ANTI-AMERICANISM?

buster movie think only of what they've seen in the movie, and they have no knowledge of this background story. As a result, some people are criticizing the ROK government for never having awarded Kim Won-bong with some sort of patriot medal of merit. That shows the terrifying power of movies in manipulating public opinion.

On September 7, 2016, the Korean film industry — that is accused of leaning towards the Left — released yet another movie that glorified Kim Won-bong: The Age of Shadows. This movie also scored a big box-office hit with a record 7.5 million ticket sales. Interestingly enough, Kim Won-bong was played by another A-lister star actor Lee Byung-hun. Lee Byung-hun is a popular actor in Korea and even in Hollywood who starred in "G.I. Joe 2," "Red 2," "Terminator Genesis," and "Magnificent 7". It was less than a year after the release of Assassin that the Korean movie industry channeled its energy into glorifying Kim Won-bong by bringing in one of the biggest Korean stars, Lee Byung-hun, to play his role.

North Korea claims Kim Il-sung led the Battle of Pochonbo, an anti-Japanese independence campaign. It is to idolize Kim Il-sung.

Anti-Japanese sentiment — like anti-American sentiment — plays a significant role in unifying people, and does it so easily, because movies can make people bond together with one ideology by using the hatred towards someone, even though individually they may have different thoughts and come from different living and educational backgrounds. The anti-Japan code motivates people to build a sense of identity as one nation and leads them to the idea that the South and the North should fight against Japan as one instead of fighting each other. Perhaps "glorifying Kim Won-bong" might have been just the first step. So, now the question is: "Who will be the next?" Arguable, maybe, but before long, we might even witness the release of a Korean movie where Kim Il-sung is glorified as an anti-Japanese independence movement fighter, as claimed by the North.

The anti-Japanese sentiment has always been a subject of controversy even in the sports field where there should be no political controversy. On 25 January 2011, Ki Sung-yueng scored the opening goal during the

Ki Sung-yueng performed a "monkey ceremony" after scoring the opening goal during the 2011 AFC Asian Cup match between South Korea and Japan.

1. WHY ANTI-AMERICANISM?

The screenshot of the Scottish Sun

2011 AFC Asian Cup semi-final match in Qatar between South Korea and Japan. However, he created a controversy by performing a goal celebration in which he mimicked a monkey by scratching his left cheek. Some people in the Republic of Korea use the term "monkey" when mocking Japanese people. There are many Japanese who know this as a fact. When it sparked fury even in Korea, Ki defended his performance by explaining that he had performed the "monkey ceremony" in retaliation after he spotted the Rising Sun flag, a symbol of Japanese imperialism, in the stands. But it remains unconfirmed whether or not there was a Rising Sun flag in the stadium during the Korea-Japan match in Qatar. In connection with his performance, the British daily newspaper The Scottish Sun strongly criticized Ki Sung-yueng, calling him "Cheeky MonKi."

It would have been great if it all ended with this incident. But it did not. I cannot tell who's to blame for this, but Koreans' anti-Japanese sentiment doesn't show signs of dying. At the 2012 London Olympics, the Korean soccer team gave an amazing performance. Being the Olympics

Park Jong-woo performed a "Dokdo ceremony" to celebrate the victory in the 2012 London Olympics soccer match between South Korea and Japan.

host, Great Britain put together its first-ever joint British soccer team that represented Wales, Northern Island, and Scotland. For this reason, Britain — as well as the entire world — showed a keen interest in this united British soccer team. South Korea met the British team in the quarter-finals on August 4, 2012 and won a dramatic victory with a penalty kick. South Korea went on to defeat Brazil by 3-0 in the quarter-finals, and on August 10, 2012, the South Korean team made it to the bronze medal match. It was the first challenge for a bronze medal in Korean soccer history. However, as destiny would have it, the South Korean team had to play against Japan in the semi-final. In the end, the Korean team defeated Japan by 2-0 and won the bronze medal. The thrilling moment of victory, however, was soon followed by an incident that created a controversy again.

It happened when the South Korean national soccer player Park Jong-woo celebrated the victory by running across the stadium holding up a banner that read "Dokdo is our territory". Are the Japanese soccer players

1. WHY ANTI-AMERICANISM?

involved in the territorial dispute over Dokdo? Why was he compelled to display the sign with a slogan that read "Dokdo is our territory" in an Olympic soccer game? It was an incident that testified to how rampantly the absurd hostility towards Japan is spreading and emotionally affecting Koreans. In the aftermath of the incident, the International Olympic Committee (IOC) suspended awarding the bronze medal to Park Jong-woo and carried out an investigation of the incident. During this process, some people feared that the Korean national team might lose the bronze medal because of Park Jong-woo's action. South Korea should have been in a festive mood, celebrating the first-ever bronze medal in Korean soccer history, but Park's action pretty much killed off the festive mood of the historic victory.

1-5.
MOON JAE-IN ADMINISTRATION'S ATTEMPT TO ERASE THE RHEE SYNG-MAN ADMINISTRATION

On December 16, 2017, President Moon Jae-in visited the site of the Provisional Government of the Republic of Korea in Chongqing, China. President Moon had a moment of silence in front of the bust of Kim Gu, before meeting the descendants of independent movement activists. In this meeting, President Moon said.

"The Provisional Government is the roots and mantle of the Republic of Korea. The Constitution stipulates that the Republic of Korea inherits the mantle of the Provisional Government. I perceive the establishment of a Provisional Government as the beginning of the founding of the Republic of Korea."

"2019 will mark the 100th anniversary of the March 1st Independence Movement, and it also commemorates the 100th anniversary of the founding of the Republic of Korea."

President Moon's statements sparked controversy in Korea over the

1. WHY ANTI-AMERICANISM?

Rhee Syng-man (l.) and Kim Gu (r.) led Korea's independence movement mostly in America and China, respectively.

national foundation again. According to President Moon's statements, the founding father of the Republic of Korea is not Rhee Syng-man. Rhee Syng-man is a leading figure in Korea's independence movement along with Kim Gu. While Kim Gu engaged in the independence movement mostly in China, Rhee Syng-man was part of it mostly in the United States.

Rhee Syng-man moved to the United States in November 1904 to petition for the independence of Korea. While in the US, he studied at George Washington University and Harvard University, before he obtained a Ph.D. in international politics from Princeton University. On September 6, 1919, he was appointed interim president of the Provisional Government of the Republic of Korea in Shanghai, China, and beginning in December 1920, he served as an acting president of the Provisional Government for six months. In May 1920, he returned to the United States and continued his independence movement activities. Then on August 15, 1945, the Korean peninsula was liberated from imperialist Japanese rule, and Rhee Syng-man was sworn in as the inaugural president of the Republic of Korea on July 24, 1948. Some analysts pointed out that even though the Special Investigation Committee of Antinational Activists (SICAA) was formed to purge those who had been involved in pro-Japanese activities during the Japanese colonial days, President Rhee sabotaged their activities in the wake of growing conflict within South Korea. When the Korean War broke out on June 25, 1950, President Rhee stood up and fought strongly against the North and the Chinese Communist Party with the US and UN forces. Then Rhee implicated himself in the rigged presidential election on March 15, 1960 and was later forced to resign from his presidency on April 26 soon after the April 19 Student Revolution. Eventually, Rhee moved to Hawaii on May 29, 1960, and died a lonely death on July 19, 1965, in Honolulu, Hawaii. Due to various complicated circumstances, Rhee has been under constant attack from the left-wing camp in connection with issues related to pro-Japanese, pro-American activities and the rigged election, even though he is admired as the founding father of the Republic of Korea in the right-

Rhee Syng-man, the inaugural president of the Republic of Korea, was forced to resign from his presidency.

wing camp.

The position of the right-wing camp on this issue is that the Republic of Korea was established on August 15, 1948, when President Rhee declared the national foundation after he was sworn in as President on July 24, 1948, in the South Korean Constitutional Assembly. This is because it is in 1948 that all three requirements of a nation — people, territory and sovereignty — were satisfied. On the other hand, the left-wing camp claims that the national foundation day should be April 11, 1919, when the Provisional Government was established in Shanghai, China.

President Moon Jae-in fueled the national foundation day controversy again on July 3, 2018. Just prior, on June 23, 2018, President Moon Jae-in became the country's first leader to watch a national soccer team's World Cup match overseas. He visited Rostov Arena in Rostov-on-Don, Russia, to watch South Korea's match against Mexico and returned to Korea in the evening of June 24. Then he allegedly suffered from a cold and did not engage in any activity for the following seven days until July 1. During this period, he did not attend any official events either, such as the 68th anniversary of the Korean War on June 25, memorial service for the UN veterans of the Korean War on June 26, and 16th memorial ceremony for the Battle of Yeonpyeong on June 29. His absence made some people suspicious that President Moon used a cold and sickness as an excuse to miss those events, because he was conscious of the South's relations with the North. The first outside official event that President Moon participated in since his absence was the launching ceremony of the "Committee for Commemorating the 100th Anniversary of the March 1st Independence Movement and the Establishment of the Provisional

Moon Jae-in, the current President of the Republic of Korea

Government of the Republic of Korea" on July 3.

In his speech at the ceremony, President Moon stated, "We have a proud 100-year history of a democratic republic." He then stressed, "The Provisional Government is the root of the Republic of Korea." President Moon also announced that the South and the North would jointly host events to commemorate the March 1st Independence Movement. Even if the two Koreas celebrate the 100th anniversary of the independence movement, I doubt it will lead both the South and the North to agree on the 100th anniversary of the establishment of the Republic of Korea, because North Korea has been celebrating on September 9th with big events as their *de facto* national foundation day, since Kim Il-sung's regime was established on September 9th, 1948. It is deeply unnerving that while North Korea is continuing the legitimacy of the Kim Il-sung regime, South Korea just keep undermining the legitimacy of the Rhee Syng-man administration.

2. KOREA'S CORE ANTI-AMERICAN GROUP, THE "386 GENERATION"

Some people claim that now, the "386 generation" should be called the "586 generation." The term "386 generation" first appeared in 1997 as a reference to those who were in their 30s, started college in the 1980s, and were born in the 1960s. Now that 20 years have passed, and they are in their 50s, they should be called the "586 generation," people claim. But I will continue to use the term "386 generation" for this group of people because, if we follow this rule, we might have to continuously change the term to ""686 generation", "786 generation"', and "886 generation."

2-1.
ANTI-AMERICAN MOVEMENT STARTED IN GWANGJU

On April 19, 1985, Han Kyung, an English-major student at Chonnam University who chaired the "Committee for the Investigation of the Truth of the May 18 Uprising," held the US responsible for "having turned blind eyes to the massacre committed in Gwangju", and cried out, "Yankee Go Home." The "Yankee Go Home" that started in Gwangju spread throughout the country.

The scene of the Busan American Cultural Service building arson.

2. KOREA'S CORE ANTI-AMERICAN GROUP, THE "386 GENERATION"

On March 18, 1982, the American Cultural Service building in Busan went up in flames. The fire was started by a few college students from the Busan area. They claimed the United States government had approved the massacre in Gwangju. The arson attack killed a Dong-A University student who was studying in the library inside the building and left three other Dong-A University students injured. Interesting enough, the defense lawyers for the accused arsonists were Roh Moo-hyun and Moon Jae-in. This tragic incident gave them an opportunity to become power players in the Korean politics later on.

2-2.
1987 JUNE UPRISING AND NL

In 2017, a movie was released in Korea with the title of "1987".

In the movie "1987", an incident occurred that made the term "democratization movement" become widely popular in Korea. It was a large-scale demonstration that came to be known as the June Uprising, because it took place between June 10 and June 29, 1987. The protesters claimed 5 million had participated in the demonstrations, and the police

The poster of the movie "1987"

estimated the number was about 82,000.

Interestingly enough, the big difference in the number of protesters as claimed by the protesters and the police repeated in the so-called "Candlelight Rallies" that began in 2016. This kind of discrepancy has a long history in Korea. That is the reason the Korean media outlets have been including numbers claimed by both sides when they report how many people have participated in demonstrations. But such a longstanding, customary reporting practice disappeared in news reports about the 2016 Candlelight Rally. It was a situation where the news media outlets thought it was okay to ignore a fact that is important in reporting truth, which is their main responsibility. It was beginning at this time that practically all media outlets started using the number of candlelight protesters claimed only by the protesters themselves as if it was fact. Under this circumstance, it reached the point where we get to hear that a staggering 10 million people have allegedly participated in ten candlelight rallies. Does this number even make sense? The entire population of Korea is about 50 million, and according to news reports, one fifth of the entire population have participated in the demonstrations that happened only ten times. But it was really difficult to find any news outlet that raised questions about the number.

There is something we have to do before getting into further discussion about the 1987 June Uprising: a fundamental examination of the ideologies behind the so-called Democratization Movement. In Korea, student movements are largely attributed to two communist factions: National Liberation (NL) and People's Democracy (PD). NL advocates national liberation and puts emphasis on the importance of cooperating with North Korea in order to ensure genuine independence of the Korean

June Uprising in Korea

peninsula from foreign forces. For that reason, NL is also called Juche ideology faction or Juche faction. Even within NL, there are Juche ideologists and non-Juche ideologists. On the contrary, PD advocates people's democracy and distance themselves from the North's Juche ideology. However, PD follows the Marxism-Leninism ideology, and it models after the laborer-centric Soviet revolution. It is alleged that until 1987, student movements were geared more heavily towards PD than NL. Probably that was because students were repulsive about North Korea. But it is an undisputable fact that beginning from the June Uprising in 1987, the center of gravity shifted rapidly from PD to NL.

The Left is known to unite well in times of crisis and break apart in times of peace. That's the reason both NL and PD could unite and fight for the common cause during the June Uprising. Then they went their separate ways once the June Uprising was over. This pattern appeared again in 2011 when NL and PD were able to unite and launch the infamous "Unified Progressive Party" together in preparation for the upcoming 19th general election and the 18th presidential election. In the election, the United Progressive Party won 13 seats and became the third largest party within the National Assembly. However, PD raised suspicion of an illegal election during the proportional representation race. They claimed the election was rigged by NL to work in their favor. The conflict between the two factions blew up into violence. In the end, the National Assembly members that belonged to PD left the party 9 months after its establishment, thereby significantly reducing the number of Unified Progressive Party seats from 13 to five. Later on, NL kept the United Progressive Party as it was, while PD established and moved to the new party called Justice Party. The United Progressive Party, which was dominated by those from NL, was eventually disbanded by the constitutional court in 2014 on charges of having violated national security law and having plotted a rebellion.

I explain their genealogy in detail because this background story is important in understanding the June Uprising. The "June Uprising" was sparked by the torturing death of Park Jong-chul, a linguistics student at Seoul National University who was taken to the police where he was tortured and killed the very next day in January 1987. The police at the time were interrogating him to find out the whereabouts of Park Jong-woon, a sociology student at the same university. In today's world, it is hard to imagine a young student getting tortured and killed by the police. Both Park Jong-chul and Park Jong-woon were the PD ideologists who dreamt of a laborer-centered, Soviet-style communist revolution. They were students who distanced themselves from the North Korean Juche Ideology or the NL ideology.

Up until this incident, PD was the mainstream of student movements. Then an opportunity came to NL. PD distrusted politicians in general, and therefore were disapproving of the New Democratic Party that was led by Kim Dae-jung and Kim Young-sam. PD only dreamt of laborer-centered revolution. Then NL discovered a way to survive on their own: NL joined in the fight for an amendment to the constitution, calling for a direct presidential election system, which was exactly what the New Democratic Party was demanding. It was in 1987. Which raises the question: Why did the June Uprising start five months after Park Jong-chul's torture death that happened in January that year? And why was it led by NL, a relatively minority group of ideologists, and not by PD, the victim of the incident and the mainstream of student movements at the time? It was because NL joined forces with the New Democratic Party to demand amendment of the constitution and a direct presidential election system.

According to Park Chan-soo's *Modern History of NL*, PD, which was the mainstream at the time, was reluctant to join forces with reformist politicians who they believed were not interested in solving fundamental problems of social structure. PD regarded that as a sign of "populism" or 'popularism'. On the other hand, NL was able to grab public attention by crying out such popular slogans as "Stop the Attempts to Protect the Constitution" and "Down with Dictatorship." The analysis tells us that NL was able to grab the upper hand in student movements because it chose to take a more flexible, popular route.

When you think about it, it is quite ironic that the tragic death of a PD student eventually blew up into the June Uprising and ended up weakening the influence of PD and empowering its rival, NL, instead.

There are people who believe that the government's incompetent response might have made the uprising worse than it had to be. It started with the torture death of Park Jong-chul, but the final straw was a photo that surfaced on June 9, 1987. In the photo, Yi Han-yeol, a public administration student at Yonsei University, was seriously injured — with blood trickling down his head and the life already gone from his eyes.

He was injured after a tear gas shell penetrated his skull when the riot police fired tear gas at the group of students demonstrating in front of Yonsei University. It was truly a ridiculous thing to happen. The police were supposed to fire tear gas at an upward angle, but they shot it directly towards people on a horizontal angle. I cannot believe the police made such a ridiculous mistake when confronting young students. Yi was transferred to a hospital, and died on July 5, 1987, less than a month later.

I myself have childhood memories of the 1980s. I remember the city of Seoul always being clouded with the smoke from tear gas. Today, Seoul is now suffering from fine dust and yellow dust originating from China, but back in the 1980s, Seoul was suffering from tear gas. Smoke from tear gas doesn't kill people. But the police clearly did wrong in the case of the student. Intended or not, having the tear gas shell hit and kill a per-

Funeral procession for Yi Han-yeol who was killed by the shell of a tear gas fired by the riot police during the June Uprising.

son was something that should never have happened.

The June Uprising began on June 10, 1987, which was the day the ruling Democratic Justice Party was having a convention to nominate their presidential candidate. The June Uprising did not start on June 10 because Yi Han-yeol was seriously injured by the tear gas shell on June 9. A large-scale demonstration was already scheduled before the incident, but the demonstration had a higher turnout than originally expected because of the incident.

The government made another mistake: They requested that companies send their employees home earlier because they were concerned a large-scale student demonstration would result in serious congestion in the city. On top of that, the government made subway trains pass stations in the mid-town areas in order to prevent students from taking subways to come to the center of the city. In 2016, the subways also skipped mid-town stations near the areas of demonstrations when the candlelight rallies were going on. But in this case, it was not intended to stop the demonstrators from entering the center of the city; I believe it was out of safety concern resulting from a large crowd swarming to subway stations all at once. June 10, 1987 was a Wednesday. Thanks to the government's consideration, workers could leave their job earlier than usual. But that left them with time on their hands because they did not have anything specific to do as it was a weekday, not a weekend. Besides, the workers whose jobs were in mid-town areas could not take subways to go home either. All these circumstances came together to create the perfect conditions for them to naturally turn to and participate in the June Uprising. The June Uprising, led by the NL ideologists, was a huge success largely because a massive number of workers — who came to be known as "Neck-tie Battalions" — were able to join the demonstration.

2. KOREA'S CORE ANTI-AMERICAN GROUP, THE "386 GENERATION"

People say "if" doesn't mean anything in history. But I cannot help but wonder what the Republic of Korea would be like today "if" the government did not make the workers leave their jobs earlier, or "if" President Park Geun-hye did not make a statement apologizing to the people the very next morning after JTBC aired a report about Choi Soon-sil and her tablet late at night on October 24, 2016. How would it have changed the South-North relations if it did not happen, and what would have happened to Korea-US relations? I cannot stop asking "if" and thinking about possible scenarios, because a small decision can end up changing history.

The June Uprising of 1987 left a strong impression on people's minds because it resulted in the June 29 Declaration in which Roh Tae-woo — the then-presidential candidate of the ruling Democratic Justice Party and the second in power within the party following President Chun Doo-hwan — promised to amend the constitution to provide for the direct election of the president, instead of the current indirect system.

The massive group of demonstrators cheered at this, because it meant they fought and defeated the military regime. In the meantime, a new form of activist groups that was completely different from those of the existing and former politicians started to form, during which the NL activists emerged as the core power group within the left-wing camp.

It was around 1997 that the term "386 generation" began to emerge. It was about ten years after the June Uprising that happened in June 1987. The term "386 generation" refers to those who were in their 30s, started college in the 1980s, and were born in the 1960s. For that reason, some people claim that they should be called "586 generation" instead of "386 generation" because 20 years have passed now and they are in their 50s, not 30s, today. But I will continue to use the term "386 generation" for this group of people because that's the term that defines that specific group of people, even though it is slightly illogical. And I am focusing on this group of people defined as the "386 generation" because the 386 generation is unleashing significant influence in the current Moon Jae-in administration.

PD started losing its hegemony to NL after the June Uprising in 1987, NL has been the voice of the left-wing camp for over 30 years since it emerged as the core power group within the anti-government demonstrators.

Previously I've mentioned how PD lost its hegemony to NL by refusing to proactively participate in the New Democratic Party's campaign to amend the constitution because they did not approve Kim Dae-jung and Kim Young-sam. It shows how activist groups are basically in a relationship of little trust with existing politicians. Therefore, even though the Kim Dae-jung and Roh Moo-hyun administrations are both leaning towards the Left, there is a slight difference between the two. As we are all aware, President Moon Jae-in was the former secretary general in the Roh Moo-hyun administration. Therefore, the Moon Jae-in and Roh Moo-hyun administrations have a slightly different significance from the Kim Dae-jung administration as well. It was beginning with the Roh Moo-hyun administration that the "386 generation" made their forays into politics, thereby allowing those from NL to emerge as the mainstream politicians. And from these politicians started the real anti-American and pro-North Korean sentiments. And today, they are seizing almost all the important posts within the Moon Jae-in administration.

Lately, there has been a heated controversy over the key figures of the Moon Jae-in administration and whether they can be defined as *Juche* faction or "*Jusapa*" in Korean — a shortened term of *Juchesasangpa* which refers to a movement that supports the North Korean political ideology known as Juche ideology. On November 6, 2017, during the parliamentary inspection of the administration, lawmaker Chun Hee-kyung from the Liberty Korea Party stated, "Cheongwadae (Blue House) is dominated by *Jusapa*, Then the Chief Presidential Secretary of the 1st secretarial staff Im Jong-seok protested and said, "I feel very insulted." Some people denounce the argument over *Juche* faction or *Jusapa* as an outdated ideological orientation. They claim it is comparable to the US arguing about "McCarthyism" in the 21st century. The problem, however, is that it's far from being an outdated argument. The term *Jusapa* is not synonymous with the commonly used derogatory term "commies." It refers to the people who came from the NL political camps. Then one can only wonder why they feel insulted when they are referred to as "*Jusapa*" if it is true that they are from the NL political camps. All I can say is that it seems to be their attempt to treat the term "*Jusapa*" as a taboo and prevent the term itself from even being mentioned.

2-3.
AN INCIDENT THAT SHOWED HOW TERRIFYING NL REALLY IS

There might be many criteria for distinguishing between NL and PD, and even more complicated sub-criteria as well in that matter. But simply put, PD dreams of a working-class revolution in support of Leninism, while NL is all about struggling to accomplish independence of the country from all foreign forces based on the principle of anti-Americanism. For NL, the core values are anti-Americanism and unification. From this perspective, NL is divided again into *Jusapa* and non-*Jusapa*, depending whether one is supporting the *Juche* Ideology perfected by Kim Jong-il of the North, or acknowledging the North's Workers Party as the leadership of the Republic of Korea transformation movement. Given that, there is no question North Korea has a significant role in NL. On December 19, 2014, the Constitutional Court of the Republic of Korea delivered a ruling that forced the disbanding of a party called the Unified Progressive Party (UPP). It was the first time the ROK Constitutional Court had ever ordered a political party to disband. The ruling also stripped parliamentary seats from its lawmakers, namely, Oh Byung-yun, Lee Seok-ki, Kim Jae-yeon, Kim Mi-hee and Lee Sang-gyu, effective immediately.

2. KOREA'S CORE ANTI-AMERICAN GROUP, THE "386 GENERATION"

The UPP is a party created on December 6, 2011 through a merger of the Democratic Labor Party, the People's Participation Party, and the Alliance for the Creation of New Progressive Party. That's how the party was born out of a grand union of those from both the NL and PD activist groups. In the general election of the National Assembly that took place on April 11, 2012, the UPP formed an alliance with the Democratic Party and nominated a single presidential candidate for better odds to defeat the right-wing Saenuri Party candidate. In this election, the UPP won 13 seats, thereby becoming the third largest party within the National Assembly behind the Saenuri Party and Democratic United Party. After the general election was over, however, internal conflict occurred over the illegitimate proportional primary, which resulted in growing tension between the NL and PD groups. Eventually, the lawmakers from PD left the UPP and created a new Justice Party on October 21, 2012.

The UPP became a party dominated by the NL lawmakers, who became involved in a conspiracy to commit treason in August 2013. The National Intelligence Service conducted an investigation into a revolutionary organization called RO run by Lee Seok-ki, and pressed charges against the organization for having conspired and incited rebellion and violating the National Security Law and others after the organization was discovered to have attempted a socialist revolution with the goal of overthrowing the Korean government. Lee Seok-ki was arrested because he was found to have instructed the RO team members, "The revolution is coming. Prepare to raid communications and oil storage facilities and railroads." And for the first time in the history of the Constitution, the Justice Department filed a petition requesting that the Constitutional Court dissolve the UPP.

On May 12, 2013, Lee called 130 members of revolutionary organization (RO) to the auditorium of " The Marist Brothers Korea". which is situated in Hapjeong-dong, Mapo-gu, Seoul. At the meeting, the organization members discussed specific rebellion-related plans which included plans to bomb the oil storage facilities in Pyeongtaek, Gyeonggi Province, and the destruction of communications facilities at KT branch in Hyehwa-dong, Jongno-gu, Seoul. A lot of people were shocked to find out about these activities when the recording of their meeting was made public by the National Intelligence Service (NIS). It turned out that the meeting was secretly recorded by somebody known only as Mr. Lee, a former RO member, at the request of NIS. On January 22, 2015, the Supreme Court found Lee Seok-ki guilty of having violated the National Security Law and plotting treason and sentenced him to nine years in prison and 7 year suspension of license.

Earlier on December 19, 2014, the Constitutional Court delivered a ruling that ordered the dissolution of the UPP, stating that the party was found to have a propensity for a broad sense of socialism that reflects socialist ideals and values of the North Korean regime and a means to carry out the North's revolutionary strategy against South Korea. It was an 8-1 vote in favor by eight out of nine judges. This case made a lot of Koreans scared about the NL activist groups.

After Lee Seok-ki's arrest, the National Assembly investigated the activities that Lee Seok-ki had engaged in while a member of the National Assembly. It turned out Lee Seok-ki had proactively requested confidential military documents by taking advantage of his parliament membership. He had requested 30 confidential military documents, most of which were about U.S. forces stationed in Korea. The documents Lee Seok-ki had requested from the Ministry of Defense included those about the Korea-US joint military exercises, purchase of weapons, the second runway at Pyeongtaek Osan Base, and Korea-U.S. military cost-sharing. The case was a wake-up call that made us realize what dangerous things could happen when an extremely anti-American person from NL becomes a member of the National Assembly.

3. NOTABLE EXAMPLES OF ANTI-AMERICAN MOVEMENT

3-1.
TERRORISM ATTACK AGAINST THE OFFICIAL RESIDENCE OF THE US AMBASSADOR TO KOREA

After NL became the center of student movements in the wake of the June Uprising of 1987, the anti-American movement started picking up in full swing. On October 13, 1989, an activist group named "Anti-American Death-defying National Salvation Corps," which was affiliated with the National Council of Student Representatives, raided and took over the official residence of the US Ambassador to Korea. This incident was selected as one of the major anti-American violence cases in the report titled "Political Violence Against Americans," which was published by the US Department of State in August 2013. It started when six college students who belonged to the National Council of Student Representatives broke into the US Ambassador to Korea's official residence located in Jeong-dong, Jung-gu, Seoul, by stepping on a vehicle and jumping over the fence. One of the students was Jung Chung-rae, who later joined the Democratic Party and served two terms as a member of the National Assembly. As soon as they jumped over the fence, they detonated a homemade bomb, and when the security guards rushed in at the sound of the explosion, they detonated the second homemade bomb.

Then they smashed the window and entered the living room, and cried out, "Go Home, US Ambassador Donald Gregg!" They built a barricade with chairs they'd found in the house and poured paint thinner before setting them on fire as well. During this process, several valuable artworks including antiques were damaged. Ambassador Gregg and his wife were able to avoid the danger by quickly escaping through the window to the house next door. It was an act of terrorism where homemade bombs were used at the official residence of the US Ambassador to Korea, but Jung Chung-rae , who took a part in the act, was sentenced to only six years in prison. Later, Jung Chung-rae confided that the punishment was lighter than he had expected. They even received special amnesty from the Kim Young-sam administration in 1995. And Jung Chung-rae went on to become a member of the National Assembly. The case clearly leaves us feeling bitter, because such a slap-on-the-wrist punishment for terrorism against the US Ambassador to Korea can result in undesirable consequences. One can say it created a bad precedent. Eventually, on March 5, 2015, another US Ambassador to Korea, Mark Lippert, was attacked and had his face slashed with a 25cm long knife. I will explain this case in further detail later.

3-2.
PRESIDENT-ELECT KIM DAE-JUNG AND THE FULL-FLEDGED MOVEMENT OF 386 GENERATION

Kim Dae-jung won the presidential election on December 18, 1997 and became the 15th President of South Korea. His victory marked the birth of the first-ever left-leaning government since the founding of the Republic of Korea. Previously I've mentioned how the term "386 generation" was born in 1997. Now that the Korea's first left-wing administration was born after years of right-wing administrations, sweeping changes of personnel in major government posts were inevitable. During this process, the "386 generation" who were pretty young at the time took over major government posts in the Kim Dae-jung administration.

Deeply rooted in the hearts of the political figures from NL that was the major force behind the June Uprising on 1987 was hostility against the United States, because they believed the United States has been supporting the right-wing administrations of South Korea for a long time. According to David Straub's *Anti-Americanism in Democratizing South Korea*, the Korean media reported one after another rumor about the misconduct committed by the US soldiers stationed in Korea, but the Korean journalists did not bother to check the source of such information properly or handle them objectively. David Straub believed that the Korean news media was extremely critical about the United States Forces Korea (USFK) because in 1999, a significant number of newspaper reporters and opinion editors were "386 generation." Since Kim Dae-jung took office, many left-wing activist groups received support from the government. During the process, NGOs that blatantly targeted the US troops stationed in Korea, such as the Headquarters of the Withdrawal of USFK Movement and the National Campaign for Eradication of Crimes by U.S. Troops in Korea grew bigger. In the end, it resulted in a situation where the 386 generation entered a smooth collaborating relationship with the Korean news media that reported various suspicions on the USFK whenever they were raised by these anti-American NGOs.

3-3.

NO GUN RI INCIDENT, US TROOPS IN KOREA, AND THE MOVIE 'HOST'

Since the inception of the Kim Dae-jung administration, the Korea-US relations have been worse than ever. A report that came out in 1999 about the No Gun Ri Incident seemed to symbolize the Korea-US relationship that was gradually tanking. The incident is about the US soldiers having slaughtered Korean war refugees between July 26 and 29, 1950 during the Korean War. US fighter planes allegedly shelled towards the Korean refugees gathered at a railroad bridge near the village of Nogun-ri, Yeongdong-gun, North Chungcheong Province, killing hundreds of them. The incident was investigated by a Korea-US joint committee, that could not corroborate the claim that the US soldiers had intentionally slaughtered Korean civilians in a situation where disguised North Korean soldiers were suspected to have infiltrated the refugee groups. The No Gun Ri Incident was the beginning of the anti-American movement.

Since then, left-leaning environmental NGOs in South Korea continued to hold hostile sentiment toward the USFK. On September 30, 1999, the Vietnam War Veterans Association filed a civil lawsuit in a Korean court against the South Korean and US governments and a US company that manufactured an herbicide and defoliant chemical called Agent Orange. But a suggestion was made that the various sicknesses the victims were suffering from might have been caused by factors other than the defoliant alone, such as smoking or drinking, because too many years had passed since they were exposed to the defoliating agents.

Then on July 13, 2000, the Green Korea announced that USFK secretly released a toxic chemical known as formaldehyde into the Han River, which was the source of drinking water for Seoul citizens. The group claimed that Albert McFarland, a US Army funeral officer, forced his employees to release 60 gallons of formaldehyde into the river. Later on, hundreds of protesters threw rocks at the US military bases in Yongsan and revealed their hostility towards the US soldiers. The anti-American public sentiment that was triggered by the Agent Orange and the formaldehyde incidents was fueled all over again when the director Bong Joon-ho released the movie "Host" in July 2006. This movie was a big box-office hit that recorded over 10 million ticket sales. The movie begins with a scene where a US soldier discharges formaldehyde into the Han River, which later causes the fish to transform into a huge monster and kill people. And the name of the chemical people use to kill the monster in the movie is Agent Yellow. It was a movie that blatantly displayed raw anti-American sentiment, as if to show that the movie maker was incapable of using metaphor in a subtler way.

3-4.
APOLO ANTON OHNO AND THE ANTI-AMERICAN MOVEMENT

The 2002 Salt Lake City Winter Olympics that took place from February 8 to 24 in Utah, USA, is an event that I really don't want to think about because of what happened in the Korea-US relationship as a consequence. It poured oil on Koreans' hatred against the United States at a time when the anti-American sentiment was already flourishing under the Kim Dae-jung's administration. The Ohno Incident, as most Koreans remember it, happened on February 20, 2002 during the men's 1,500 short track race. The Korean speed skater Kim Dong-sung was expected to win the gold medal at the game, and his rival Apolo Anton Ohno was a star skater from America. As we all remember, Kim Dong-sung was speeding with the finish in sight with Ohno closely behind when Ohno attempted to overtake Kim. During this process, Ohno threw up his hands as if he was pushed and lost balance. The referee ruled that Kim had interfered with Ohno, and disqualified Kim for the violation. Since Kim Dong-sung was convinced he had won the gold medal and responded to the cheering fans holding up a Korean flag, the disqualification decision came as a shock to everybody in Korea. Soon Koreans started revealing anti-

3. NOTABLE EXAMPLES OF ANTI-AMERICAN MOVEMENT

American sentiment as they made complaints and comments, claiming that the US bribed the referee or forcefully robbed Kim of his gold medal. The fact that Anton Ohno was a half-Japanese, half-American served as a catalyst to further infuriate Koreans, because in Korea, anti-Japanese sentiment is just as sensitive an issue as anti-American sentiment.

Four months after the "Ohno Incident" came the World Cup games in Korea. Luck had it that Korea and the US teams belonged to the same group in the qualification match. The match between the Korean and US teams kicked off on June 20, 2002 in Daegu, and Korean soccer player Ahn Jung-hwan scored a dramatic goal to earn a draw against the USA. Then Ahn Jung-hwan celebrated the goal by mimicking a speedskater, to which another player Lee Chun-soo responded by mimicking what Anton Ohno did. This goal celebration sent many Koreans wild because they believed Korea had settled the score with the United States with that performance.

Two Korean national soccer players Lee Chun-soo and Ahn Jung-hwan are mimicking the US speed skater Anton Ohno after scoring a goal on June 10, 2002.

3-5.
THE WORST TRAFFIC ACCIDENT AND CANDLELIGHT RALLIES

On the morning of June 13, 2002, two middle school students Shim Mi-seon and Shin Hyo-soon were walking along the 57th provincial road in Yangju, Gyeonggi Province, on their way to meet friends. Yangju is a city that is situated somewhere between Seoul and the DMZ. It was a Thursday, and one might wonder why these two middle school students were going to their friend's house in the morning instead of going to school. They didn't have school that day, because it was the 3rd nationwide local election day. So the two middle school girls were enjoying an off-school day. In this election, the right-wing Grand National Party (GNP) won 11 seats and the left-wing Millennium Democratic Party (MDP) won 4 seats at the metropolitan municipality election. In the local election, GNP won 140 seats while MDP won only 44 seats. It was the day when the right-wing political party made a landslide victory. Unfortunately, however, an incident that happened on this day completely turned Korea upside down. An armored vehicle from the 2nd Infantry Division of United States Army steered to the right lane trying to avoid another vehicle that was coming from the opposite direction, only to

3. NOTABLE EXAMPLES OF ANTI-AMERICAN MOVEMENT

strike and kill the two school girls. It was a tragic accident in which two middle school girls were crushed to death by a US Army armored vehicle. This incident triggered and climaxed the anti-American sentiment that had gotten steadily worse since the inception of the Kim Dae-jung administration.

The USFK prosecutor charged the drivers of the vehicle, Sergeant Mark Walker and the vehicle's commander Sergeant Fernando Nino, with "negligent homicide." The case was tried at the US military court located in Camp Casey — which is a USFK base in Dongducheon, Gyeonggi Province — and Sergeants Nino and Walker were found "not guilty" on November 20 and November 22 by two separate panels whose verdicts indicated it was a tragic accident that happened while conducting official duty without criminal culpability. Those who'd been claiming the two US soldiers had committed a capital crime were enraged at the acquittal verdict and took it to the streets. And a large-scale candlelight rally was held on November 26, 2002 in Gwanghwamun. Koreans were used to coming to the plaza since Korea hosted the 2002 World Cup games. In the case of the June Uprising of 1987, they needed to be armed with invincible spirit of resistance, but beginning in 2002, their demonstrations became more like festive events. According to David Straub's *Anti-Americanism in Democratizing South Korea*, left-leaning activist organizations including some of the anti-American NGOs "took the lead in politicizing tragedy." In his memoir published in 2009, Thomas Hubbard, the then-US Ambassador to Korea, stated, "Koreans were enraged at the way the US handled the tragic death of the schoolgirls, and this played a critical role in President Roh Moo-hyun's victory in the election." In a massive-scale demonstration of over 100 thousand protesters that took place on December 14, the protesters ripped up the Stars and Stripes. This incident was said to have

Psy smashed a model US tank in protest of the US military during his concert in 2002. He made an official apology in 2012.

aired on major TV channels throughout the United States and shocked many Americans.

On November 29, 2002, the Korean singer Psy, whose "Gangnam Style" made him an international celebrity, gave a performance that would not be forgotten in the memory of many people. It was during a Mnet KM music festival called "2002 MMF" which was a big event considered to be the biggest festival in Korea and even in Asia. The event has been called MAMA since 2009 when its name was changed to Mnet Asian Music Awards. Psy was performing on stage during this event when suddenly he picked up a model armored vehicle and threw it down onto the stage floor. Then he swung the microphone stand as if it was a steel pipe and started striking the armored vehicle model. A Korean national flag was tied to the microphone stand. Fast-forward ten years in 2012, Psy sent fans from around the world wild with his song "Gangnam Style." But what he did back in 2002 put him in hot water. When the American media raised questions about his past behavior, Psy made an official apology on December 8, 2012.

This whole incident shows how rampant the anti-American sentiment really was in Korea. However, the hatred fever cooled down quickly. The year 2002 was truly a year marked by a series of dynamic events. In February 2002, there was the Salt Lake City Winter Olympics, in June, there was Korea-Japan World Cup soccer match, and in December, there was a presidential election. It is amazing how all these major events were colored with anti-American sentiment. The 16th presidential election was held on December 19, 2002, where the presidential candidate from the left-wing camp, Roh Moo-hyun, was elected by a narrow margin by winning 49% of votes in a race against the right-wing camp candidate Lee Hoi-chang who won 47% of votes. After this election, the number of people who participated in candlelight rallies quickly dropped from several tens of thousands to just several thousands, and within just a few days, the number went down again to just a few hundreds. Straub analyzed that, after the election was over, the leftists changed their direction to ease

Roh Moo-hyun won the presidential election in 2002.

the conflict with the US to help the new Roh Moo-hyun administration now that they accomplished the election of a left-leaning president, even though the left political parties and NGOs strongly criticized the US when the presidential election was fast approaching. Straub also pointed out that the Korean news media didn't feel the need to report more about the two schoolgirls since the public's interest in the incident cooled after Roh Moo-hyun's victory, and that there was also the influence of Roh Moo-hyun, who allegedly requested the media to go easy on criticizing the USFK.

3-6.

CALLOUS TO THE BATTLE OF YEONPYEONG? POLITICAL MOTIVATION CONTROVERSY

Korea was badly shaken up in the aftermath of the Yangju Highway Incident that happened on June 13, 2002. It had such a tremendous impact on the Korean people that many of them joined anti-American demonstrations and criticized the US However, people paid little attention to an incredible incident that occurred on June 29, 2002, just 16 days later: the Battle of Yeonpyeong.

If somebody asked where the powder keg of Korea was, I would say it is Yeonpyeong-do, a small island that belongs to Ongjin-gun, Incheon, just off the coast of Hwanghae Province of North Korea. The waters surrounding the island have been a frequent cause of conflict with North Korea. The problem is that it is hard to draw clear lines of demarcation in the ocean, unlike the land where there are clear boundaries such as the 38th parallel and DMZ. The conflict between the South and the North was frequently over the Northern Limit Line known as the NLL. The NLL is a maritime demarcation line in the West Sea established by the Commander of UN Forces, Mark W. Clark, immediately after the end of the Korean War in 1953. For the next 20 years, North Korea did not raise questions over the line that was set by the United Nations Command (UNC). Then beginning in October 1973, the North started ignoring the NLL and kept crossing the line, consequently causing problems. But never did the situation escalate to a fatal skirmish.

It all changed on June 29, 2002, at 10:25 am, when two North Korean patrol boats opened fire on a South Korean Chamsuri-class patrol boat while the entire country was swept up in a festive mood watching the Korea-Japan World Cup match. A shootout followed that lasted for a staggering 31 minutes between the South and the North Korean patrol vessels, causing the South Korean patrol boat named Chamsuri 357 to sink, causing 18 casualties including the deaths of Lt. Cmdr. Yoon Young-ha, Petty Officer Han Sang-guk and four other soldiers, and 18 injuries. The North Korea vessel reportedly sustained 30 casualties as the result of the ROK Navy's return fire. It was a serious military clash but, having happened during a World Cup game, the battle did not create a big stir. Shocking as it is, President Kim Dae-jung had reportedly left for Yokohama, Japan, the day after the battle, to watch the World Cup final match between Korea and Japan. That means President Kim chose to watch the Brazilian king of soccer Ronaldo scoring a goal against the German team and cheering for him instead of visiting and paying respect to the Korean soldiers including Lt. Cmdr. Yoon who had lost their lives in the battle. But people didn't consider it a major issue, because back then, no Korean news media channel criticized President Kim in connection with this issue. However, the movie "Battle of Yeonpyeong" that was released on June 24, 2015, had a scene that criticized the President's whereabouts, if only indirectly. In the movie, Lt. Cmdr. Yoon's father is at his son's wake when he turns to TV and briefly watches President Kim leaving for Japan to watch the World Cup match. Honestly, it is very unusual that such a

3. NOTABLE EXAMPLES OF ANTI-AMERICAN MOVEMENT

President Kim Dae-jung left for Japan to watch the World Cup final match the day after the Battle of Yeonpyeong.

movie was even made and released considering how the Korean movie industry is dominated by leftists. What is surprising is that, despite all kinds of cynical and negative reviews of leftist movie critics, the movie recorded over six million ticket sales. It was a box office success. On the Naver movie review website, over 6,500 moviegoers participated in the rating and gave it 9.14 out of a perfect score of 10. On the other hand, four movie critics gave it an average rating of a mere 4.94, demonstrating the big contrast between the two sides.

There is no life in the world that is not precious. It is heartbreaking that two schoolgirls were run over by a US Army's armored vehicle and crushed to death, and it is also heartbreaking that six South Korean soldiers were shot to death by soldiers on the North Korean patrol boats. All males born in South Korea are required to serve in the military unless they are exempt for special reasons, because by law, they all have the obligation to serve the country. The death of the soldiers — not career soldiers, but soldiers who died while fulfilling their duty to serve the country — was a heartbreak shared by all mothers who had sons born in the country, and also a heartbreak shared by all young Korean men as well. However, I cannot help but feel bitter when I think about the anti-American rallies where anger boiled over on November 26 and December 14 in 2002 in connection with the incident involving two schoolgirls, Hyo-soon and Mi-seon, and then how quickly the anti-American fever cooled down after the presidential election was over on December 19. Clearly, both were tragic incidents, but the suspicion cannot be shaken off that the left-wing political parties and citizen groups have used those tragic incidents for their own political purposes.

Kim Han-na, the wife of Lt. Cmdr. Han Sang-guk who was killed in the Battle of Yeonpyeong, was so angry and disappointed at how callous the Roh Moo-hyun administration was about the soldiers who died in the line of duty that she left Korea and moved to the United States in April 2005. She returned to Korea only after the government organized a ceremony to officially commemorate the fallen soldiers for the first time in April 2008 when the right-leaning Lee Myung-bak administration began. Her story speaks volumes about what the Battle of Yeonpyeong meant to the left-wing Kim Dae-jung and Roh Moo-hyun governments.

There is another famous story about President Roh Moo-hyun on this subject. It came to light when Dailian published an article on June 29, 2008. According to the article, a senior Korean government official visited Washington DC in preparation for President Roh Moo-hyun's visit to the US slated in May 2003 and had a meeting with the US Secretary of State Condoleezza Rice. Secretary Rice asked him, "Do you know the names of the schoolgirls who were hit and killed by the US armored vehicle?" The official immediately answered, "They were Hyo-soon and Mi-seon." Then Rice asked him, "Do you know the names of the soldiers who died during the battle of Yeonpyeong?" but he could not answer. Rice found it absurd and said, "How can you remember the students who were killed by the vehicle from an ally forces, but not the names of those who lost their lives fighting for their country?"

3-7.
PROTEST AGAINST U.S. BEEF

Currently, the presidential term in Korea is five years. That's the major difference from the political system of the United States, where a president is elected to a four-year term, with a limit of two terms. Coincidently, the right-wing administrations of Lee Myung-bak and Park Geun-hye share something in common: They both experienced large-scale anti-government rallies within a year after they sworn in, and they became lame ducks earlier than usual as the result of anti-government rallies that happened throughout their terms. Lee took office as president on February 25, 2008. In the parliamentary elections on April 9, the right-wing Grand National Party (GNP) won 153 seats out of 299 available in the National Assembly, while the left-wing Democratic Party won only 81 seats, making it a landslide victory for the GNP. I've already mentioned how the conservative GNP made a sweeping victory in the local election on June 13, 2002. I want to refresh your memory that in the same year, there were massive anti-American rallies in connection with the deaths of Hyo-soon and Mi-seon, and how it gave momentum for the left-wing presidential candidate Roh Moo-hyun to win in the presidential election.

3. NOTABLE EXAMPLES OF ANTI-AMERICAN MOVEMENT

It is interesting how the Mad Cow disease report broke when all conditions were working in favor of a right-wing government at the time. I believe this development is the best example to show the growing anti-Americanism of Korean news media, because in this case, anti-American rallies were sparked as the result of an issue created by the news media, as opposed to the past when it was the aftermath of unfortunate incidents. On April 29, 2008, Korea's second largest national TV network MBC aired a shocking investigative report on a program called *PD Notebook*, which was made by MBC producers who were heavily leaning towards the Left even within the already left-leaning broadcasting company. Titled "US Beef, Is It Really Safe from Mad Cow Disease?" the report raised issues on the Lee Myung-bak administration's negotiation over the import of US Beef in connection with Korea-US FTA, claiming that the administration allowed beef from US cattle that had a high risk of Mad Cow disease. This was just two months after the inception of the Lee Myung-bak administration. The previous President, Roh Moo-hyun, agreed to import US beef from cattle less than 30 months old only, but President

Korea reached agreement with the US to import beef from US cattle.

Lee agreed to import US beef from cattle over 30 months old at the request of the US President George Bush, the program claimed. South Korean negotiators reached agreement with the US on this rule and others about beef imports about ten days earlier on April 18, 2008.

Kim Bo-seul, one of the producers of the program, located the family of Aretha Vinson in Portsmouth, Virginia, USA. The 22-year-old Aretha Vinson had undergone a gastrectomy at Maryview Medical Center on Jan. 23, 2008 to treat obesity. After the surgery, she showed symptoms including nausea and vomiting, and on February 26, she was admitted to Maryview Medical Center again and remained hospitalized for ten days for treatment. Then on April 2, she received treatments for symptoms including dizziness and blurred vision, before being transferred to the intensive care unit of the hospital on April 5 after complaining of difficulty breathing. A few days later on April 9, she died.

The problem was the translation of the interview the *PD Notebook*

A screenshot of MBC report on the death of Aretha Vinson.

staff had with Aretha Vinson's mother. The key was whether Aretha died of CJD (Creutzfeldt Jakob disease) or vCJD (variant Creutzfeldt Jakob disease). CJD is a fatal degenerative brain disorder and vCJD, also known as the human version of Mad Cow disease, is a separate one from the latter. In the interview, Aretha's mother Robin Vinson said, "Doctors suspect Aretha has Creutzfeldt-Jakob (CJD)." But the conclusive-tone of the translated subtitle in the *PD Notebook* read, "According to doctors, Aretha was diagnosed with vCJD, which is a variant Creutzfeldt Jakob disease." I leave the verdict to the readers on this.

In the same interview, Robin Vinson said, "According to MRI results, I was told there was a possibility that Aretha had CJD," but in the translated Korean subtitle, "CJD" was replaced with "vCJD". According to a report by Munhwa Ilbo on July 2, 2008, the translator of this episode of *PD Notebook*, Chung Ji-min, strongly criticized the *PD Notebook* production crew for the clear mistranslation, claiming, "I translated this part correctly as 'CJD' but somebody had intentionally changed it to 'vCJD'." But this new development came to light two months after the program aired, during which time too much damage had been already done to Korea.

After the program was aired, ungrounded horror stories quickly spread throughout Korea, including "Eating US beef leaves your brains perforated," and citizens came out to the Gwanghwamun Plaza and rallied in protest of the US beef imports. Candlelight rallies started on May 2 and lasted for 106 days, during which period the police estimated over 980,000 people came to rally. In the beginning, they were non-violent rallies by people who were truly concerned about health issues, but later on, they escalated into violent, illegal, anti-government protests that left the area around Gwanghwamun a scene of total anarchy. At the time,

Numerous concerned citizens joined the candlelight rallies against the import of the US beef.

President Lee Myung-bak reportedly went up to a mountain behind the presidential Blue House and shed tears looking at the candlelight rally that was going on at the Gwanghwamun Plaza. With the "Mad Cow disease" frenzy that started just three months after the inauguration of the President, the Lee Myung-bak administration lost the momentum to push forward with reformist policies designed to make a transition from the previous left-wing administration to his right-wing administration in the early days in office.

The irresponsible comments made by celebrities also contributed to the people's US beef scare. Actress Kim Min-seon, for example, declared "I would rather drink cyanide than eat the US beef." I cannot tell if the heated controversy that followed her statement had anything to do with it, but later, Kim Min-seon changed her name to Kim Gyu-ri. By the way, Kim Min-seon was caught entering In-N-Out Burger chain in Los Angeles and devouring a hamburger, and this was exposed on the TV show "Trend Report Feel Season 2" that was aired on March 18, 2009. It

3. NOTABLE EXAMPLES OF ANTI-AMERICAN MOVEMENT

made people wonder if Kim Min-seon presumed In-N-Out was not using US beef in their hamburgers.

If eating US beef truly leaves human brains perforated as they claimed, we should have heard about many cases of people who'd died of the Mad Cow disease by now. But that's how such inflammatory claims compelled a massive number of Koreans to take it to the streets and rally.

As I mentioned earlier, there were many contributing factors surrounding the death of Aretha Vinson. Her condition worsened after the gastrectomy surgery. On July 29, 2008, the Special Investigative Team of the Seoul Central District Prosecutor's Office announced the results of the on-going investigation on allegations of biased MBC *PD Notebook*. According to the prosecutor's office, MBC *PD Notebook* did not disclose the fact that Aretha Vinson had a gastrectomy surgery and did not mention the possible causes of death other than vCJD, thereby making it sound conclusive that the cause of her death was vCJD. In addition, they pointed out that, since there were as many as 59 causes that could result in the so-called "downer cow" syndrome, just because a cow cannot stand on its own does not mean the cow definitely has the Mad Cow disease.

Kim Min-seon is eating a hamburger at In-N-Out Burger.

Common sense tells me their stories simply don't add up. Aretha Vinson died in Virginia, USA. Suppose she actually died of Mad Cow disease, and Mad Cow disease is responsible for downers in the US. Then, why did Americans never rally about it? Was it because the American news media simply ignored issues surrounding Aretha Vinson? Was there any other American who died of Mad Cow disease afterwards? When you ponder these questions, you can easily find the common-sense answer to the Mad Cow disease issue.

Currently, Korean imports of US beef amount to $12.2 million, which is roughly ₩1,330 billion in Korean currency. The amount is the second largest in the world only after Japan, whose imports total $18.9 million. The total amount may be less than that of Japan, but when you consider Korea has less population than Japan, you can easily see that Koreans love US beef. According to an analysis of the US beef imports by country conducted by the Korea Rural Economic Institute, Korea turned out to have imported 3.5kg per person, followed by 2.4kg in Japan, and 1.9kg in Mexico.

In December 2010, the Seoul Central District Court ruled that the main content of the *PD Notebook* broadcast at issue was "not true." The court found it not true that: a downer was conclusively suffering from mad cow disease; the cause of death of Aretha Vinson was definitively vCJD; and the risk of getting the Mad Cow disease for Koreans when consuming beef contaminated by Mad Cow disease was 94%.

KBS and MBC are the two biggest broadcasting companies in Korea, and their presidents are practically appointed by the government. I will address this subject in detail later. Currently under the Moon Jae-in administration, the MBC president is Choi Seung-ho, who is a former current affairs TV producer who played the leading role in the production of the *PD Notebook*. Can it be just a coincidence that *PD Notebook*'s report on the Mad Cow disease dealt a critical blow to the Lee Myung-bak administration, and Choi Seung-ho — the main player behind the *PD Notebook* brouhaha — was appointed the MBC president soon after the inception of the left-wing Moon Jae-in administration?

3-8.

KNIFE ATTACK ON U.S. AMBASSADOR TO KOREA MARK LIPPERT

On March 5, 2015, US Ambassador to Korea Mark Lippert was attending a breakfast event hosted by the National Council for Reconciliation and Cooperation at Sejong Center, when a man named Kim Ki-jong lunged at the Ambassador and slashed him in several places including his face and left arm with a 10-inch knife. Ambassador Lippert was just about to have breakfast when Kim Ki-jong, who turned out to be the

US Ambassador to Korea Mark Lippert was attacked by a man.

head of an alliance of Seoul citizen cultural groups, knocked him over and started slashing him. During the attack, Kim Ki-jong cried out, "Stop the Korea-US joint military exercises!"

Ambassador Lippert was rushed to a hospital where he received 80 stitches in the face and underwent a surgery to reconnect nerves on the left wrist. The Supreme Court delivered the final decision to send the attacker to jail for 12 years on charges including attempted murder. The judge ruled, "Considering the motives and the details of his action, he is believed to have intended murder."

According to the New Daily report on March 6, 2015, Kim Ki-jong was also head of an organization named "Urimadang," which is affiliated with the NL labor and cultural movement organizations, and a significant part of their activities showed pro-North Korean orientation.

4. CURRENT SITUATION OF ANTI-AMERICAN ACTIVISTS IN THE MOON JAE-IN ADMINISTRATION

The June Uprising of 1987 provided an opportunity for NL that was somewhat associated with North Korea to become the center of student movements. PD that followed the Marxism-Leninism ideology had to watch how NL was growing its influence.

Eventually, NL gained momentum in the wake of the wildly successful June Uprising and went on to form the National Council of Student Representatives, also known as Jeondaehyop, in August. On August 19, 1987, the National Council of Student Representatives (NCSR) had its inaugural ceremony at Chungnam National University with over 4,000 college students representing 95 colleges from around the country attending. The name of the person who spearheaded this development was Lee In-young. Lee was the chairman of the Korea University Students Association, and he immediately became the first president of the NCSR. Later on, Lee joined the Democratic Party in 2004 and became a member of the 17th National Assembly. He is currently still serving this third term after winning seats for the 19th and 20th National Assembly.

4-1.
NATIONAL COUNCIL OF STUDENT REPRESENTATIVES — WHAT DO THEY DO?

NCSR is the most important organization to understand the people working for the Moon Jae-in's government. NCSR followed the "National Liberation People's Democratic Revolution (NLPDR)" ideology when it formed the "anti-American frontline for the national liberation and unification of Korea." Pompous as the title may sound, we need to talk about what NLPDR is really about.

In 1970, North Korean leader Kim Il-sung delivered the "Instruction on the National Liberation People's Democratic Revolution" at the 5th party convention as follows:

"South Korea is a colonial anti-capitalist society where its sovereignty and means of production are in the hands of US imperialists, its comprador capitalists, land owners, and reactionary bureaucrats."

"The South Korean Revolution is a national liberation revolution to fight against the invading US imperialist forces, while at the same time, the people's democratic revolution to oppose land owners who are there as running dogs for the United States, comprador capitalists, and reactionary bureaucrats, as well as their fascist politics."

In 1988, the headquarters of the national police explained the NLPDR that NCSR is following. It said:

"The National Liberation People's Democratic Revolution is an ideological line believing in the struggle against anti-American national independence and anti-fascist democratic movement, and it is mirroring the North Korean regime's national liberation people's democratic revolution which is the North's revolutionary campaign for the communization of South Korea."

That means, NLPDR is the main goal of the NCSR to follow the North's revolutionary strategy to form an anti-American frontline for the national liberation and unification so that they can make USFK withdraw from the Korean Peninsula and expel the American imperialist and right-wing government, until they can establish a pro-North democratic government for the people in the South. And their final target is the foundation of a socialist nation through the federalist-based reunification with the North.

NCSR followed the North's three campaign strategies of independence, democracy and unification, and defined South Korean society as "a capitalist society colonized by the US imperialists."

4-2.
POLITICIANS FROM THE NATIONAL COUNCIL OF STUDENT REPRESENTATIVES (NL)

Currently, there is a person who is recognized as wielding the most power in Korea. He is not the Prime Minister or the Minister of Strategy and Finance who serves as the deputy prime minister for economic affairs. It is Im Jong-seok, who is the Chief Presidential Secretary of the 1st secretarial staff at the presidential Blue House. All previous Chief Presidential Secretaries have been close aides to the President, but they did not involve themselves in politics outside the President's office. But Im Jong-seok has been acting completely different from his predecessors. He is so involved that practically everything he says or does makes the news, thereby making people call him the real power in the Blue House. For this reason, there are people who predict that Im Jong-seok will become the next presidential candidate after Ahn Hee-jung — the former South Chungcheong Governor who was considered as the next presidential candidate to succeed President Moon Jae-in — took a fall as the result of allegations that he had sexually abused his female secretary.

Im served as the 3rd president of NCSR in 1989. Even though

4. CURRENT SITUATION OF ANTI-AMERICAN ACTIVISTS IN THE MOON JAE-IN ADMINISTRATION

Im Jong-seok, the Chief Presidential Secretary of the 1st secretarial staff at the presidential BlueHouse.

NCSR was established soon after the June Uprising in 1987, the NCSR did not have its own office or executive functions till its second year. But the NCSR became much more powerful beginning in its third year when it opened an office in Hanyang University Student Hall in March 1989.

It is interesting how the NCSR opened an office in Hanyang University. NCSR was headed by students from Korea University in its first and second year, as we can see the first president (Lee In-gi, president of the Korea University Student Association) and the second president (Oh Young-sik, president of the Korea University Student Association). Up until that time, everybody accepted it as a matter of fact that the heads of nationwide college student movements had to be students from Seoul University, Korea University, or Yonsei University. In Korea, these three top colleges are called SKY, which is coined by taking the initials of the three colleges. The word SKY became synonymous with the most prestigious colleges in Korea. However, when a student from PD became the president of Yonsei University Student Association and a similar situation happened at Korea University where PD became as influential as NL in the campus, Hanyang University emerged as the school to provide the candidate to hold leadership in NL. At that time, NL was the dominating power in Hanyang University, Kyunghee University, and Konkuk University. Under the circumstances, it is alleged that Hanyang University implicitly supported Im Jong-seok to become the NCSR president. The university allowed the NCSR to open an office on the campus, believing that it was an opportunity for the university to improve its status in the college rank that was dominated by Seoul National University, Korea University and Yonsei University at the time.

Eventually, Im Jong-seok was elected as third president of the nationwide college student body NCSR, and he demonstrated he had much stronger power than previous NCSR presidents. When Im showed up at the NCSR convention, tens of thousands of students rose from their seats and gave him a standing ovation, chanting "Iron-strong Invincible Council for the Salvation of Nation" and singing the "NCSR March Song". According to Park Chan-soo's *Modern History of NL*, this kind of hype that the NCSR showered on Im had something to do with the unique culture of NL, which made much account of authority. But even within the left-wing camp, there were people criticizing it as being overboard for young students. The characteristic of the NL activists is that, internally, they emphasized authority and discipline to the point where it looks excessive, but outwardly, they put the demands of the public as their top priority and make their moves with flexibility.

At that time, the NCSR unleashed tremendous power. In the opinion poll conducted by the current affairs magazine Sisa Journal in 1990, the NCSR ranked number three among the "organizations that move South Korea" after the ruling Democratic Liberal Party and the opposition Peace Democratic Party. The NCSR outranked even the Federation of Korean Industries whose members included such large corporations as Samsung, LG, and Hyundai.

4. CURRENT SITUATION OF ANTI-AMERICAN ACTIVISTS IN THE MOON JAE-IN ADMINISTRATION

More than anything, Im Jong-seok shocked a lot of Koreans when he was found to have been the leading figure who helped another fellow college student, Lim Su-kyung, make an illegal trip to North Korea without obtaining permission from the South Korean government. According to the report titled "Is the National Council of Student Representatives an Organization of Innocent College Students?," which was released by the Ministry of Safety and Planning (currently NIS) in 1991, North Korea hosted an event called the World Festival of Youth and Students in Pyongyang in June 1989, and Im Jong-seok discussed Lim's participation at the Festival over the phone with the head of the North Korean Joseon Student Committee who was staying in Vienna, Austria, at the time and the organizing director of the League of Socialist Working Youth of Korea Central Committee.

At that time, the photos of Lim Su-Kyung hugging Kim Il-sung shocked numerous people. Lim Su-kyung went to Japan, first alleging that she was a tourist, before flying to East Berlin in East Germany, from

Lim Su-kyung (r.) and Kim Il-sung (l.). Their meeting was orchestrated by Im Jong-seok, the Chief Presidential Secretary of the 1st secretarial staff at the presidential BlueHouse.

Im Jong-seok is in prison uniform as he is taken away.

where she was able to fly to North Korea. After the festival was over, Lim Su-kyung came back to South Korea on foot by walking past Panmunjom. This incident is recorded as the first case of a civilian college student openly coming from the North to the South since the Korean War in 1950. As was expected, she was arrested for having violated the national security laws and was sentenced to five years in prison. Fast-forward to 2012, she was elected a member of the National Assembly as a proportional representative of the Democratic Party.

As the prime culprit responsible for Lim Su-kyung's illegal trip to the North, Im Jong-seok was also sent to prison for five years on charges including the violation of natural security laws. Im Jong-seok is famous for his firm anti-American ideology. According to the Hankyoreh newspaper article dated October 15, 1989, he claimed "The anti-American struggle is the key to the struggle for national unification." In another article by Dong-A Ilbo dated September 22, 1989, he also stated, "the United States has been causing tremendous suffering for Koreans through politi-

4. CURRENT SITUATION OF ANTI-AMERICAN ACTIVISTS IN THE MOON JAE-IN ADMINISTRATION

cal maneuvering and economic extortion." According to the prosecutor's indictment of Im Jong-seok — which Hankyoreh printed on February 2 7, 1990 — Im Jong-seok argued, "Sharing many things in common with the North's claims can make reunification happen earlier than later, don't you think?" And he blatantly declared "I uphold the unification policy that is in line with that of the North." He also chaired a committee for the Inter-Korean Economic & Cultural Cooperation Foundation in 2006, which I will discuss in detail in the next section.

In addition to Im Jong-seok, there are many former NCSR members who currently hold important positions in the Blue House. President Moon's speechwriter Shin Dong-ho was the first director of culture at NCSR and the chief commissioner of the Inter-Korean Economic & Cultural Cooperation Foundation in 2004. He'd also been in charge of paying royalties for news materials to the North while serving as director of South-North Copyright Center, which is affiliated with the Foundation, in 2006. The funny part about this position is that, if a news media channel in South Korea such as a broadcasting company used a video clip made by the North's Korean Central Television (KCTV), they have to pay royalties for that to the Inter-Korean Economics & Cultural Cooperation Foundation. It makes me wonder on what grounds this organization is acting as the agency for the North and collecting royalties for copyright in South Korea for the North. According to the statistics by the Ministry of Unification that Joongang Daily reported on July 19, 2017, the Center sent over $2 million to the North over a span of 13 years. As of 2010, money transfer to the North was banned after the May 24 measures imposed by the South's government against the North after 46 seamen from the ROK Navy were killed by gunfire from the North Korean corvette.

A screenshot of the North's Korean Central Television report criticizing the South Korean government.

But the Foundation is ready to start sending money to the North as soon as this measure is lifted. Considering how things are going in the Moon Jae-in's government, it seems that the ban will be lifted sooner than later.

Baek Won-woo, the Presidential Secretary for Civil Affairs, is the former executive secretary of NCSR and has been advocating the abolition of the national security law and reduced US military forces in Korea during the eight years he was a member of the National Assembly starting in 2004. He'd sent a complaint to the US Embassy in Korea on September 2, 2004, in protest of the US Congress having passed a bill about North Korean human rights.

President Moon's close aide Song In-bae is the former president of Pusan National University Student Association, and he was also a member of the 5th NCSR. During the initiation ceremony of this 5th NCSR that took place at Pusan National University in May 1991, a US national flag was burned.

4. CURRENT SITUATION OF ANTI-AMERICAN ACTIVISTS IN THE MOON JAE-IN ADMINISTRATION

Student members of the South Korean Federation of University Students Council broke into a US base in Korea and attempted to burn down a US flag. A US soldier is trying to stop them.

A US flag is being burned by protesters.

Song In-bae had also claimed, "The United States is carrying out an imperialistic aggression" while protesting the government's decision to dispatch our troops to the Gulf War as the acting president of the Busan and Ulsan branch Council of Student Associations on February 19, 1991.

4-3.
POLITICIANS FROM NON-NCSR ORGANIZATIONS (PD)

Just because somebody is from a non-NCSR or NL organization doesn't mean the person is pro-American, or against the North's dictatorship regime. NL and PD are different only in terms of methodological approach. They are peas in a pod when it comes to their anti-America, pro-North political orientations.

Beginning in 1997, college student associations in Korea started to elect for their presidents those who were not from a student movement

An anti-American politician Kim Sang-gon. He is the current Minister of Education.

4. CURRENT SITUATION OF ANTI-AMERICAN ACTIVISTS IN THE MOON JAE-IN ADMINISTRATION

Senior Presidential Secretary for Civil Affairs Cho Kuk, a PD politician.

activist background. Up to that point, a president of any university student association was a student movement activist without exception. Kim Sang-gon was the President of Seoul National University Student Association in 1971 and is currently the Minister of Education. The Ministry of Education in Korea is considered the deputy prime minister of social affairs, and ranks number four in the Cabinet after President, Prime Minister and the Deputy Prime Minister of Economic Affairs. Kim Sang-gon made an appearance in court as a witness during the trial, because he was implicated in the "Seoul National University Students' Conspiracy for Treason Case," which was exposed by South Korea's Central Intelligence Agency (current National Intelligence Service: NIS) on November 13, 1971. And on March 24, 2008, he also claimed "USFK should withdraw and the Korea-US alliance has to be abolished."

Senior Presidential Secretary for Civil Affairs Cho Kuk is the one who founded the Seoul Social Science Research Institute with alumni who were admitted to Seoul National University in 1982, the same year as him. He researched the Soviet's Marxist political economy and contributed to building the theoretical foundation for the PD student movement activists to distinguish them from the NL activists. Cho Kuk was arrested in 1993 on charges of having participated in the South Korean Socialist Laborers Federation incident. South Korean Socialist Laborers Federation (SKSLF) was established in 1988 with the goal of socialist revolution by means of armed uprising. According to the investigation report made public by Korea's Central Intelligence Agency (current National Information Service), on April 3, 1992, the mastermind of the SKSLF incident, Park No-hae, was found to have attempted to raise an armed force to accomplish a revolution by instigating workers to stage protests for higher wages, before convincing them to carry out a general strike and elevating strikes into a struggle for political revolution.

The Presidential Senior Secretary for Social Innovation, Ha Seung-chang, was once arrested for having violated the National Security Act on April 28, 1990, and his arrest was connected to the incident involving the Workers' Federation for the National Unification and Democracy. Ha Seung-chang established the Federation with colleagues and carried out activities intended to turn workers from Gyeonggi Province and Incheon areas into left-wing ideologists. It is reported that his organization denied the existing order of liberal democracy and aimed to build a communist regime in the South by accomplishing class revolution through armed uprising.

| 4-4.

MINBYUN, A LAWYERS' SOCIETY ALIGNING ITSELF WITH LEFT-WING GOVERNMENT

On August 21, 2017, President Moon Jae-in nominated Kim Myung-soo, the chief judge of Chuncheon District Court, as the new Supreme Court chief justice. Kim Myung-soo is the former President of the International Human Rights Law Society, which was formerly known as Our Law Society established by leftist judges. That means the Moon Jae-in government nominated one of the leading left-wing judges as the chief justice to be true to their nature of being a left-wing government.

Then on July 2, 2018, Chief Justice Kim Myung-soo nominated lawyer Kim Seon-soo as a candidate for Supreme Court justice. While Our Law Society and the International Human Rights Law Society are organizations of leftist judges, Minbyun, or the Lawyers for a Democratic Society in English, is famous for being an organization of leftist lawyers. Kim Seon-soo was appointed the President of Minbyun in 2010, and in 2014, he was the lead defense attorney for the Unified Progressive Party when the party was tried at the Constitutional Court in 2014. As I've mentioned previously, the Constitutional Court issued a ruling in an 8-1 decision to dissolve the UPP on the grounds that the UPP had a propensity for a socialism that reflected socialist ideals and values of the North Korean regime.

A former lawyer Moon Jae-in was also a member of Minbyun, which was created by a merger of the Justice Serving Lawyers' Club and Young Lawyers Club in 1988, a development spearheaded by lawyer Cho Young-rae. Originally, Minbyun was a small group of 51 members only, but it began to thrive when the member lawyers were appointed to important government positions during the Roh Moo-hyun administration. For years, Minbyun has been advocating campaigns of the left-wing camp such as the abolition of the National Security Act and refusal to relocate the US military base in Pyeongtaek, but they took and argued cases for various organizations that benefit the enemy including the case of Wang-jaesan, which was an underground political group who allegedly pledged allegiance to Kim Il-sung and spied for North Korea. For this reason, Minbyun has been criticized for "destroying national identity and human rights under the pretext of protecting them."

In the liberal democratic system, jurisdiction, administration, and legislation have to be clearly distinguished. The jurisdiction part, in particular, has to be independent from political power. However, President Moon Jae-in appointed left-leaning Kim Myung-soo as the Supreme Court chief justice, and Kim Myung-soo himself nominated left-leaning Kim Seon-soo as a Supreme Court judge. What would the future of Korea if even the jurisdiction is handed over to the Left?

Besides, Minbyun has a problem beyond just being a left-wing organization. It was Minbyun member lawyer Chang Kyung-wook who defended Lee Seok-ki in a trial when UPP member Lee Seok-ki was suspected of having conspired to overthrow the government, which I explained earlier. Lee Seok-ki was arrested because he was found to have instructed the RO team members, "The revolution is coming. Prepare to raid communications and oil storage facilities and railroads." The Supreme Court found Lee Seok-ki guilty of having violated the National Security Act and plotting treason and sentenced him to nine years in prison and 7-year suspension of license.

Chang Kyung-wook also took the case of the Wangjaesan spy group incident in 2011. According to the Chosun Ilbo article dated November 27, 2013, Chang Kyung-wook visited a professor who was the key witness in the case, before the authorities had a chance to interrogate him, and asked, "If they bring you in for interrogation, please exercise your right to remain silent." Being a former member of the spy group Wangjaesan, the professor was a key witness who could testify about what Wangjaesan was really about.

Chang Kyung-wook was in hot water after it was exposed that, on November 12, 2013, Chang Kyung-wook attended a seminar in Potsdam, Germany, with delegates from an organization affiliated with the United Front Department — which is the North's department in charge of operations in the South — and claimed, "The US and South Korea are responsible for the instability of the Korean peninsula." We will have to wait and see how Minbyun's pro-North and anti-American ideology will influence in the Moon Jae-in government.

5.
CURRENT STATUS OF THE KOREAN MEDIA

5-1.
THE BIRTH OF THE NATIONAL UNION OF MEDIA WORKERS (NUM)

The power that moves the Korean media is not in the hands of the owners or executives of newspapers or broadcasting companies, or ordinary journalists. It is in the hands of the National Union of Media Workers (NUM) that is under the umbrella of the Korean Confederation of Trade Unions (KCTU). The origin of the National Union of Media Workers can be traced to the establishment of the Korea Federation of Press Unions in 1988, under the Federation's inaugural president, Kwon Young-ghil.

Kwon Young-ghil, the inaugural president of the Korea Federation of Press Unions.

5. CURRENT STATUS OF THE KOREAN MEDIA

Korean Confederation of Trade Unions

While working as a reporter for Seoul Shinmun, Kwon Young-ghil was in Paris as a correspondent for a whopping seven years from 1980 to 1987. In general, a foreign correspondent assignment comes with various privileges such as having your child's education and living expenses all paid for by the company, and most foreign correspondents stay 3-4 years in the respective country. But for some unknown reason, Kwon Young-ghil lived in Paris for seven years as a correspondent. I find this a little odd. Perhaps it was possible because he was a man of significant power within the company at the time.

After returning from Paris, Kwon Young-ghil immediately set out to establish the Korean Federation of Press Unions (KFPU), and the Federation had its inauguration ceremony at the Press Center International Conference Hall on November 26, 1988. Kwon Young-ghil elevated himself from the chairman of the KFPU preparatory committee to the inaugural KFPU chairman as was planned, just like Lee In-young had created NCSR and took its presidency himself.

Once established under the leadership of Kwon Young-ghil, KFPU started picking up and jumping in to struggles against the government and executives of news companies. The Ministry of Labor recommended that KFPU join the Federation of Korean Trade Unions, which is a higher-level labor organization, but KFPU refused. This refusal was only a prelude to the establishment of the Korean Confederation of Trade Unions (KCTU) which was committed to struggling much more radically than the Federation of Korean Trade Unions. It was Kwon Young-ghil who established the KCTU on November 11, 1995. As you can guess, Kwon Young-ghil became the inaugural KCTU chairman. KCTU under the leadership of Kwon Young-ghil carried out sweeping actions including a general strike, whose caliber was not even comparable to that of the Federation of Korean Trade Union. As of today, KCTU is an umbrella group of NUM, but if you look at the past, you can see that NUM was KCTU's parent union. KCTU has 16 affiliated organizations whose members have climbed to 730,000. Some of the prominent unions affiliated with KCTU include National Union of Media Workers, Korean Teachers and Education Workers Union and Korean Metal Workers' Union. In particular the NUM (National Union of Media Workers) that controls the Korean press and the Korean Teachers and Education Workers Union that controls the Korean education system are continuously growing their influence, thereby making a counter-balancing force necessary for the future of Korea.

Then one might wonder if KCTU is closer to NL or PD. Considering how PD is more about class revolution and NL is more about "nation" and "anti-Americanism," one might assume that KCTU is closer to a PD. But surprisingly, KCTU has been closer to NL. According to Park Chan-soo's *Modern History of NL*, KCTU was more influenced by NL in terms of its dedication to external growth. Since they asserted that they had to appeal to a larger crowd through the "public line," the claims made by NL played a more important role than PD did within KCTU.

On June 19, 2014 during the Park Geun-hye administration, the Seoul Administrative Court made a decision in favor of the Ministry of Labor and Employment in a lawsuit filed by the Korean Teachers and Educational Workers Union (KTU) after the Employment and Labor Minister gave notice to KTU that it was an illegal union on the grounds that nine teachers dismissed from schools still had membership. As the result of this court decision, KTU is not a legal union as of now. But after the inception of the Moon Jae-in administration, KTU has been continuously asking the government to overturn the decision about it being an illegal union. It remains to be seen if KTU will end up reinstating its legal status.

On May 25, 2017, a press reported about the Seoul Unification Hall of Seo Seoul Life Science High School in Gung-dong, Guro-gu, Seoul.

Kwon Young-ghil makes a speech during his campaign for the 1997 presidential election.

In the photo, about a half dozen high school students were sitting on the floor in a room where there were portraits of Kim Il-sung and Kim Jong-il, along with big banners that read "Dear Party, You are the Mother" and "Family of the General." Currently, there is no avenue to find out if there are KTU member teachers in the Seo Seoul Life Science High School. On April 20, 2010, lawmaker Cho Jeon-hyuk from the right-wing Liberty Korea Party disclosed the list of KTU members and the schools they belonged to. A few years later on July 24, 2014, the Supreme Court ruled that Cho Jeon-hyuk had to pay about $300,000 to the KTU members, at a rate of $100 each. The court decided that Cho Jeon-hyuk violated the privacy of the KTU members. Therefore, it is now difficult to find out where the KTU member teachers are working. However, as Seo Seoul Life Science High School showed, we are left to feel revolted to find photos of Kim Il-sung and Kim Jong-il hanging inside a school facility in the South.

Now, let me get back to the Kwon Young-ghil story. Later on, Kwon made a foray into politics and became a full-pledged politician. The

Inauguration ceremony of the Korean Confederation of Trade Unions

5. CURRENT STATUS OF THE KOREAN MEDIA

Inauguration ceremony of Media Today

Korean Confederation of Trade Unions (KCTU) that Kwon created and chaired founded a left-wing political party in 1997: People's Victory 21 Party. Immediately after founding the party did he run for the 15th presidential election in 1997. He didn't win the election, scoring just a little over 300,000 votes, which accounted for 1.2% of the total votes.

Then he went on to create another political party in 1999. This time, it was named Democratic Labor Party, which was a political party leaning a lot more to the Left than his previous People's Victory 21 Party did, and it was largely centered on workers. Again, Kwon made himself the inaugural leader of the Democratic Labor Party and went on to win a seat at the 17th National Assembly in 2004 and won again at the 18th National Assembly in 2008.

In 1995, the Korean Federation of Press Unions published its first weekly online and offline periodical, Media Today. Media Today started as a trade magazine dedicated to criticizing the press, but over the years, it expanded its range of topics until it became more like a general press magazine that covers stories about politics, economy, society, and culture. With its close ties to the KCTU and NUM, the magazine is constantly subjected to controversies over the biased articles.

Korean Federation of Press Unions was established in 1988, but 12 years later in 2000, the name was changed to National Union of Media Workers (NUM). The first chairman of the union after it changed the name was Choi Moon-soon.

Choi Moon-soon graduated from Kangwon National University with a major in English Education, before joining MBC where he mostly covered social affairs as a member of the mobile investigative reporting team. It is alleged that, while working for MBC, he was not a stand-out reporter, which is in contrast to Kwon Young-ghil who was privileged to be a correspondent to Paris for seven years while working for Seoul Shinmun. In 1998, Choi Moon-soon served the Korean Federation of Press Unions as the 6th chairman and remained in that position for two years. In 2000, when the union became an affiliate of Korean Confederation of Trade Unions and changed its name to National Union of Media Workers, he became the new union's first chairman and served two more years. It means he'd chaired the union for four years in total. Even though he was not a stand-out reporter at MBC, he was on a roll within the NUM. Choi Moon-soon was not a star reporter during the left-wing Kim Daejung administration that started in 1998, or another left-wing Roh Moohyun administration that started in 2003. When he returned to MBC after his term at the NUM was over in February 2002, he was appointed the chief sub-editor of the feature reporting department and social affairs, and later, he became the sub-deputy editor of the online news reporting

5. CURRENT STATUS OF THE KOREAN MEDIA

Choi Moon-soon became the MBC president in 2005.

desk. In short, he was never in a senior position or important desk. The reporters on a roll at the time were mostly assigned to the politics, unification and foreign affairs, or business desks, and a few more successful ones had the luck to cover stories about the National Assembly, or were sent to Washington DC, New York, or Paris as correspondents.

Nevertheless, Choi Moon-soon became the MBC President in February 2005. The promotion shocked everyone. He was 48 years old at the time, thereby making him the youngest ever to become the MBC president, and it was a surprising promotion from just a sub-deputy editor to the president. He skipped all the ranks in between — sub-deputy editor, chief editor, managing editor, editor-in-chief — when he made the leap to become the president. Such an unprecedented promotion had a big impact on the change of personnel at MBC branches in Busan, Daegu, and Gwangju, not to mention of the executives at headquarters.

How can such an unprecedented promotion be possible? It might have been because it happened during the Roh Moo-hyun administration that was slightly different from the Kim Dae-jung administration. Both administrations were left-wing, but the Roh Moo-hyun's government made one after another shocking changes of personnel. On top of that, having built up influence within the NUM while serving as its chairman for four years also proved the power of Choi Moon-soon, which allowed him to jump the ranks within MBC.

So you may wonder what Choi Moon-soon did after his three-year term as the MBC president was over in February 2008. After leaving office as the president of Korea's second largest broadcasting company, he immediately joined the Democratic Party. It didn't seem to bode well that he quickly jumped into a political group after having served as the chairman of the National Union of Media Workers and then the president of the broadcasting company during the Roh Moo-hyun administration. It showed how the responsibility of the press to remain neutral and fair was thoroughly ignored. In 2008, he won a seat at the 18th National Assembly, and in 2011, he ran for Gangwon Province governor and became the 36th governor of Gangwon Province. He is still the governor of Gangwon Province after winning at the 37th and 38th governor elections.

He is a good example that gives us insight into the birth and the growth of the National Union of Media Workers.

The following is a brief history of National Union of Media Workers.

1988	Establishment of the Korean Federation of Press Unions (First Chairman Kwon Young-ghil)
1990	Company-wide strike at KBS
1992	MBC Strike

5. CURRENT STATUS OF THE KOREAN MEDIA

1995	Establishment of the press critic magazine "Media Today"
2000	Establishment of National Union of Media Workers (First Chairman Choi Moon-soon)
2006	General strike of NUM against Korea-US FTA
2007	Establishment of media solidarity in preparation for presidential election
2008	General strike of NUM against the personnel appointment by orders from the top
2009	Second and third general strikes against the suppression of the press
2012	General strike of news media outlets to demand the right to unbiased news coverage (MBC, KBS, YTN, Yonhap News, Kookmin Daily)
2015	Demonstration for the resignation of President Park Geun-hye following her political scandal
2017	Struggle to eradicate deep-rooted corruption in the press

National Union of Media Workers on a strike.

This brief history shows how NUM cared more about politically-charged strikes and struggles than about the interest and wellbeing of the union members. The 2012 general strike of news media outlets to demand the right for unbiased news coverage makes us wonder how they define "unbiased news coverage." Can we really trust the "unbiased news coverage" claimed by NUM that is under the umbrella of the Korea Confederation of Trade Unions? And no other examples can prove the bias of news media outlets more than their rally to demand the resignation of President Park Geun-hye that happened in 2016.

5-2.
ONE OF THE MOST RADICAL UNION'S STRIKE IN MBC

MBC has one of the most radical unions among all National Union of Media Worker branches that are under the umbrella of Korea Confederation of Trade Unions. KBC and MBC are public broadcasting companies whose ownership is in the hands of the people. However, this is an extremely dangerous structure. It is a structure where their presidents change whenever a new government is installed because the people are the owners. Which raises the question: Why is KBS union not as radical as the MBC union? First off, the two broadcasting companies are different beginning with their history. In the case of MBC, a *de facto* union was formed on December 9, 1987. And in the case of KBS, the KBS Labor Union has been serving as their neutral union for decades, unlike MBC. However, a KBS branch of NUM was established on December 16, 2009, and it was elevated to KBS headquarters of NUM on January 13, 2010. More than anything, the 22 years of difference between MBC and KBS — MBC in 1987 and KBS in 2009 — show the big difference in the nature of unions between the two broadcasting companies. Sure enough, now that the KBS headquarters of NUM is growing its influ-

MBC National Union of Media Workers on a strike.

ence, it is expected that KBS will also begin to show radical struggles like MBC before long.

Be it the Left or the Right, one brave man who creates a union for the first time makes the difference. The current MBC culture was credited to one brave man who came from the Left and created a union, and that brave man's name is Shim Jae-cheol. Ironic as it is, Shim Jae-cheol has grown into a prominent political leader who once served the vice-speaker of the National Assembly and is currently a lawmaker from the right-wing Liberty Korea Party.

How many days did MBC union dedicate to strikes? According to the book *What the Broadcasters Did During the Ten Years of Left-wing Government* co-authored by Choi Do-young and Kim Kang-won, MBC was on strike for 90 days during the right-wing Roh Tae-woo administration, and 36 days during the Kim Young-sam administration. But during the left-wing Kim Dae-jung administration, MBC was on strike for only 15 days, and zero days during the Roh Moo-hyun administration. Even those strikes that they carried out during the Kim Dae-jung administration were not about criticizing the government; they were about demanding reformation of broadcasting-related laws. Then came the right-wing Lee Myung-bak administration, during which time MBC was on strike for a staggering 232 days. It means MBC was on strike for about 13% of the entire five-year term of President Lee Myung-bak. Strange as it is, there was no strike during the Park Geun-hye administration, but since the inception of the left-wing Moon Jae-in administration, MBC has been on strike for 72 days. However, in this case, it was to remove MBC President Kim Jang-gyum who was appointed during the Park Geun-hye administration. And the strike that lasted 72 days came to an end on November 14, 2017 when Kim Jang-gyum was dismissed.

Then something happened in March 2009 when Lee Myung-bak was the President. Members of the MBC headquarters of NUM made a video titled "Video Message to the World" and posted it on YouTube. The main message of the video was "Korea is a dictatorship," and it was available in English, French, Spanish, Japanese, and Chinese versions. In the video, the announcer Bang Hyun-joo stated in Chinese, "Dear 1.3 billion Chi-

A union member protester is crying in joy after learning about the dismissal of Kim Jang-gyum, which ended the union protest.

The announcer Bang Hyun-ju stated in Chinese that the democracy of the Republic of Korea was in crisis.

nese people... The democracy of the Republic of Korea is in crisis." As if it was not absurd enough that an announcer from a South Korean public broadcasting company was declaring to China that the democracy of her own country was in crisis, the production crew of the video was not punished by the government at all. It is because South Korea is not a dictatorship. Imagine what would have happened if a Chinese announcer from CCTV declared that her country was a dictatorship. I don't know if the Chinese have free access to such videos on YouTube, but the incident left me bitter because it seemed to have proved how poor the qualifications of reporters, announcers, and producers of South Korean public broadcasting company really were.

The press fulfills its mission when it delivers objective facts to readers and viewers. If the press reveals that it has certain motivation, can we truly trust it as objective journalism? Now let me address problems associated with the bias of the National Union of Media Workers and its umbrella organization, the Korea Confederation of Trade Unions.

5-3.
THE BIAS OF THE NATIONAL UNION OF MEDIA WORKERS (NUM)

The National Union of Media Workers (NUM) is a union under the umbrella of the Korean Confederation of Trade Unions (KCTU). In Korea, the biggest labor union is the Federation of Korean Trade Unions (FKTU), and the second largest is KCTU whose struggles are often more radical than those of FKTU. In terms of the Left and the Right, KCTU leans more towards the Left than FKTU. The fact that NUM is under the umbrella of KCTU shows which direction the NUM is leaning to. Besides, NUM and KCTU are in a very special relationship as we can tell from the fact that Kwon Young-ghil took the lead in the establishment of the NUM and then went on to establish the KCTU, making NUM more the incubator of KCTU.

The activities of KCTU show they haven't yet moved on from the 1980s. Even though those from the 386 generation — which had emerged as the central power in NL after the June Uprising of 1987 — are now enjoying the status of backbone of Korean society, the times have changed significantly. Given that, it is pathetic that they are still crying

Protesters are tearing up a US flag on the Independence Day on August 15, 2004.

out anti-America and pro-North statements from the "386" perspectives. Each year, left-wing organizations are staging large-scale events on August 15, Independence Day, and they always chant such slogans that are anti-America and pro-North Korea during those events, even though Korea achieved independence from Japan because the United States dropped Little Boy on Hiroshima, Japan, on August 6, 1945 and the critical blow was the bomb code named Fat Man that the United States dropped on Nagasaki, Japan, on August 9, 1945. They don't seem grateful to the numerous American soldiers who sacrificed their lives fighting against the Japanese forces during WWII. At least it is extremely unnatural to cry out anti-America propaganda on Independence Day.

On Aug. 15, 2017, an organization named "8.15 Pan-national Peace and Action" which consists of over 200 left-wing organizations including NCTU, held a pan-national rally at the Seoul City Hall plaza and demanded withdrawal from the US THAAD deployment and stopping Korea-US joint military exercises. Their main demand always targets the United States. It was a large-scale rally attended by 10,000 according to

5. CURRENT STATUS OF THE KOREAN MEDIA

the organizers, or 6,000 according to police. Originally, they had planned to form a "human strip," which was about rallying while surrounding the US Embassy, but they failed to obtain permission from the court. Instead, those who came to the rally occupied an intersection on Sejongno and Gwanghwamun Square in front of the US Embassy, and cried out "Donald Trump, take THAAD and go home!" They did not forget the performance of tearing down the US national flag either.

On August 15, 2015, left-wing organizations including KCTU had a big rally near the Marronnier Park in Jongno-gu, Seoul in commemoration of the 70th anniversary of national independence. In this rally where over 7,000 participated according to the organizers, or 5,000 according to police, they ripped a US national flag again. But this time, it was a particularly disgraceful performance, because they raised a flag that had both the Stars and Stripes of the US and the Rising Sun flag that represented the past Japanese imperialism mixed together. Don't they know how many US soldiers lost their lives during the battles against Japan in

Protesters are tearing up the flag that had the images of Stars and Stripes and the Rising Sun mixed together.

WWII? Did they forget that many young Americans had their lives cut short while fighting against the Japanese imperialists? Are they ignoring the fact that 70 years ago on August 15, Korea was able to break free from Japan thanks to the sacrifices of those young Americans? The leftwing groups including KCTU had a blast while proudly tearing up the flag that had the images of Stars and Stripes and the Rising Sun mixed together. On August 17, 2015, the New Daily criticized the rally, pointing out that their rally was the exact replica of the North Korean people's rally. According to the newspaper, it was not much different from the performance of North Korean soldiers who tramped on a US national flag on July 29, 2015 during the North Korean aeronautics contest by the KPA Air and Anti-Air Force that was held in commemoration of the 62nd anniversary of the signing of the Korean War armistice. The leftist groups didn't forget to demand the withdrawal of the USFK, stopping the Korea-US joint military exercises, and withdrawing the THAAD deployment to the Korean peninsula. I am left to wonder if there is any essential difference between their hostility towards the United States and the essential part of the North's strategies against the South.

Protesters are demanding the fairness of the press.

5. CURRENT STATUS OF THE KOREAN MEDIA

A screenshot of the National Union of Media Workers' rules and regulations.

KCTU-affiliated NUM often claim "the fairness of the press" as a means to dismiss executives that they don't approve. But considering their shameful practice, NUM is the last organization that is qualified to demand fairness of the press. It is truly a shameless claim. But the current situation being already an "unlevel playing field," voices that refute their claim are difficult to hear, while their claim is blasting through a loud speaker.

NUM brazenly discloses on their website that they have a "political committee."

The "objectives and activities of the political committee" can be found in NUM's rules and regulations. It reads:

"Aiming to strengthen our competency for political activities in accordance with the Union's creed, rules and political policies, and to politicize the working-class people through alliance with democratic and progressive political groups, the Union will carry out the following activities."

The following are the activities.

1. Educate and promote activities of progressive parties and politicize workers' groups
2. Organize workers' competency for political activities

Without a doubt, this part exposes the shameful reality of the Korean press. It reveals how they have already lost interest in being fair and neutral as we would expect from the press. It is a confession of their commitment to keeping distant from — or even a hostile relationship with — right-wing political groups and parties. The "progressive parties" that they mention refer to the left-wing political parties such as the current Democratic Party and Justice Party. As a matter of fact, they have been demonstrating more blatant activities since 2012.

On March 27, 2012, NUM signed a policy agreement with the Unified Progressive Party (UPP). This agreement happened two weeks before the general election, since the election for the 19th National Assembly

Policy agreement ceremony between Korea Union of Media Workers and the Unified Progressive Party.

Policy agreement ceremony with Moon Jae-in.

was scheduled to be on April 11, 2012. With this agreement, NUM showed the world shamelessly that the union was going to have a honeymoon relationship with a specific political party. What makes this agreement more disturbing is the fact that the UPP was the very political party that was tried at the constitutional court on charges that indicated they tried to hand over the South to the North. It was a political party that was ordered by the constitutional court in an 8-1 decision to disband on December 19, 2014.

The atrocities of NUM didn't end here. In 2017 when a presidential election had to be held on short notice after President Park Geun-hye was impeached by eight justices at the same constitutional court, NUM set off to look for another left-wing political party.

The presidential election was held on May 9, 2017, and again, on April 24, 2017, about two weeks before the election, NUM signed a policy agreement with the Democratic Party of Korea's presidential candidate Moon Jae-in.

On the very next day, on April 25, 2017, NUM signed another

Policy agreement ceremony with the Justice Party.

policy agreement: This time it was with Justice Party, the presidential candidate Shim Sang-jung's party.

The presidential election of the year was a race between three candidates: Moon Jae-in from the Democratic Party; Hong Jun-pyo from the Liberty Korea Party; and Ahn Cheol-soo from the People's Party. Of course, Moon Jae-in was ahead of Hong Jun-pyo and Ahn Cheol-soo in the poll. However, NUM showed how biased the union really was when they signed policy agreements with the Democratic Party and the Justice Party while refusing to communicate with the Liberty Korea Party and the People's Party.

How influential is NUM — a media union that proved itself for being seriously biased — in the Korean press? If you look into the structure of NUM introduced in the following part, you can see NUM is unleashing dominating power over South Korea.

5-4.
STRUCTURE OF THE NATIONAL UNION OF MEDIA WORKERS

The number of union members disclosed by the NUM is really enormous. As of February 22, 2018, the total number of union members is 12,887. There are three headquarter organizations with more than 1,000 members each; 103 branch offices with more than 30 members each; and 32 sub-branches with less than 30 members each.

National Union of Media Workers protest

It is a surprisingly enormous organization. The majority of employees working at the three largest national television networks, such as MBC and SBS, not to mention the largest TV network, KBS, are NUM members. A significant number of employees working at other broadcasting companies, such as the news channel YTN, MBN, and Yonhap News TV, are also members of NUM.

In the case of printed media, a significant number of employees working for virtually all newspaper companies except for the three largest daily newspapers, Chosun Ilbo, Joongang Daily, and Donga Ilbo have NUM membership.

One might say it is fortunate that Chosun, Joongang and Donga have no ties to NUM, but we have to realize that we are living at a time when newspaper circulation figures don't mean as much as they used to. In the last few years, people have ceased to subscribe and read news articles in printed newspapers. Most people read them on their cell phones,

A view of the Naver headquarters building

because they are passively exposed to the articles of various news media outlets that are conveniently edited and made available on such portal sites as Naver and Daum. Issues associated with Naver will be explained in further details in the next chapter.

The reason such portal sites can serve the people as media outlets is simple: the reality of the press in Korea makes it easy to be dominated by NUM.

Chosun, Joongang and Donga might boast circulation that far exceeds far other newspapers, but their influence is not much different from that of other newspapers such as Hankyoreh, Kyunghyang, and Seoul when Naver dominates the news stories.

On portal sites such as Naver, articles from Hankyoreh and Kyunghyang are often exposed on the main web page more than those from Chosun, depending on the situation.

5-5.
NAVER, A LEFT-LEANING PORTAL

In fact, in Korea, Naver is the media with the biggest influence, and Daum is the next. In Korean, Daum is a word that means "next" or "behind." Probably the name of the portal is indicating that it is destined to be the second place in a race.

The power of these two online portals is signifying that the public opinion in Korea is not subject to the scale or influence of conventional news media outlets any longer.

A mammoth portal called Naver is "lifting" articles of various news media outlets, arranging them so they deliver the information as Naver wants it, and selectively delivering them to the Korean people.

Naver is an unrivaled leader and Daum is the runner-up, but there is a slight difference in terms of their political orientation. Even though both Naver and Daum are leaning towards the Left, Daum is leaning to the Left slightly more than Naver is.

There is a man named Yoon Young-chan in the Presidential Blue

5. CURRENT STATUS OF THE KOREAN MEDIA

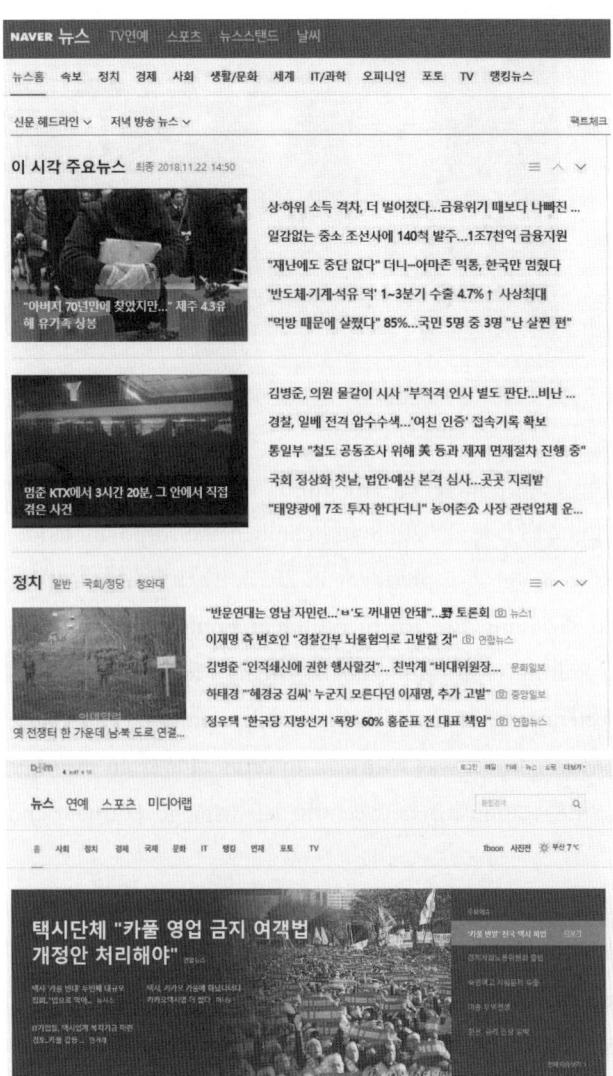

Screenshots of Naver and Daum's news feed sections

The senior secretary to the president for public communication Yoon Young-chan.

House, who is the senior secretary for public communication. Yoon Young-chan had joined Naver in 2008 and climbed the corporate ladder until he became the Naver vice president in 2013. Then in April 2017, he was appointed the joint-director of the Democratic Party of Korea Central Election Polling Committee Social Media Headquarters. He's been the senior secretary to the President for public communication since May 2017 after Moon Jae-in was sworn in to office. He is an example that clearly shows the relationship between the left-wing government and Naver.

From this case, we can easily see for what faction did Korea's most influential portal Naver edit and arrange articles from various news media outlets and deliver them to the people.

However, a much bigger scandal broke out and shook South Korea: Druking's online comments scandal.

5-6.
DRUKING SCANDAL EXPOSES THE MANIPULATION OF PUBLIC OPINION

People who use Google primarily may find it difficult to understand. Naver, the number one portal site in Korea, arranges major news items of various subjects such as politics, economy, society, and culture and shows them to their users on the main page. When users click a news item, they are allowed to write comments or click on "agree" — the Naver equivalent of Facebook's "like" — or "disagree." The problem is, the portal moves the most popular comments to the top of the comment feeds. That is the essence of the Druking Scandal.

A screenshot of comments made on Naver website. The most "liked" news article moves up to the top.

People started noticing that something was odd, because almost every article about President Moon Jae-in had a string of comments in favor of him. At least ten most liked comments were listed in the most conspicuous part, and none of those comments were criticizing him. Some people raised a suspicion that North Korea was involved in the manipulation of public opinion in the South via China in this case. Of course, this remains a possibility, because it is alleged that North Korea has an elite group of hackers called "Cyber Warriors" whose number pushes 30,000.

However, the Druking scandal was exposed to the world because of the "betrayal and revenge" of a man who was a former member of a team. On January 19, 2018, somebody posted a petition on the Blue House's online system over the suspicion of rigging comments on the news stories on Naver. According to the petitioner, somebody was constantly criticizing the Moon Jae-in administration. Eventually, the Democratic Party and Naver called for an investigation, and on April 13, 2018, the Cybercrime Division of the Seoul Metropolitan Police Department ar-

"Druking" Kim Dong-won is wearing an ear microphone.

5. CURRENT STATUS OF THE KOREAN MEDIA

The view of the Neureup Namu Publishing office.

rested Kim Dong-won, whose online user name was "Druking." Later, police discovered five people including Druking had participated in the comment rigging. Shockingly, however, all five of them turned out to be members of the Democratic Party.

The most shocking accusations usually come from insiders. As of today, Druking is accused of having rigged public opinion through Naver since the 19th presidential election in 2016. After Moon Jae-in was elected as President, he demanded that lawmaker Kim Kyung-soo — who was from the Democratic Party and a close aide to the President at the time — give him the consul-general post in Osaka, Japan as a payout. It is alleged that Kim told Druking that since somebody had already been appointed for the post, he should consider the consul-general post in Sendai, Japan, instead. But Druking was not happy about it, it is reported, and told Kim, " Sendai is a relatively small city compared to Osaka, and being close to Fukuoka, nobody wants to go there since the nuclear power plant incident." After his demand was not satisfied, Druking held a grudge against the Moon Jae-in administration and started making comments critical of it until he was arrested in connection with this not-so-funny scandal.

The most shocking accusations usually come from insiders. As of today, Druking is accused of having rigged public opinion through Naver since the 19th presidential election in 2016. After Moon Jae-in was elected as President, he demanded that lawmaker Kim Kyung-soo — who was from the Democratic Party and a close aide to the President at the time — give him the consul-general post in Osaka, Japan as a payout. It is alleged that Kim told Druking that since somebody had already been appointed for the post, he should consider the consul-general post in Sendai, Japan, instead. But Druking was not happy about it, it is reported, and told Kim, " Sendai is a relatively small city compared to Osaka, and being close to Fukushima, nobody wants to go there since the nuclear power plant incident." After his demand was not satisfied, Druking held a grudge against the Moon Jae-in administration and started making comments critical of it until he was arrested in connection with this not-so-

Kim Gyeong-su was elected governor of South Gyeongsang Province

funny scandal.

Since a special counsel has been appointed for the investigation of this case, further details are expected to come to light. As of May 7, 2018, the investigators discovered that the team used 2,290 online user names and made over 20,000 comments that were critical of the government in just two days from January 17 to 18.

After the scandal erupted, people started demanding that Kim Gyeong-su drop his bid for South Gyeongsang governor, but Kim pushed forward with his race for office, and was elected governor of South Gyeongsang Province. Of course, it remains to be seen whether he will be able to keep the post depending on the results of the special investigation.

Druking and his team were found to have used a "macro program" to automatically click the "agree" button on specific comments, which made it possible to manipulate the public opinion by making it look like a lot more people have clicked the "agree" button when it was just a handful.

Then on July 23, 2018, more breaking news shocked the entire country. Rep. Roh Hoe-chan, the floor leader of the Justice Party, jumped to his death after being suspected of having received a significant amount of political funding from Druking. Roh was originally a PD labor movement activist before he became a prominent three-term political leader in the left-wing camp. It was another tragic death associated with prosecutor's investigation following the death of the previous President Roh Moo-hyun who took his own life on May 23, 2009. Roh Hoe-chan left a note before he jumped from an apartment building in Sindang-dong, Jung-gu, Seoul. In the note, he claimed, "It is true I received money in connection with the Druking scandal, but it was not for giving him special favor."

Roh Hoe-chan took his own life.

A special team of prosecutors allegedly obtained a statement that Roh Hoe-chan received $20,000 when he visited the Neureup Namu Publishing, Paju, Gyeonggi Province, which was Druking's safe house, and that his wife also received an additional $30,000 through her chauffeur. It was also reported that the special team of prosecutors received the statement from Druking that Roh Hoe-chan was given $20,000 for a speech he delivered after participating in an event Druking had invited him to, and also secured evidence that supported this money transaction.

Druking had posted on Twitter on May 17, 2017 about the Justice Party and Roh Hoe-chan. The Justice Party has former PD activists as its core members. Druking's Twitter post read:

"Hey, the Justice Party, Shim Sang-jung and your gang... Rumor has it that you are trying to move the KCTU to tame the Moon Jae-in administration. I warn you. It takes only one punch to knock you all out cold — Shim Sang-jung and Kim Jong-dae connection, and even Roh Hoe-chan. Just keep dancing around if you don't trust me."

Shim Sang-jung is another prominent politician, who had served the leader of the Justice Party in the past and ran for the presidential election in 2017. Kim Jong-dae is also a lawmaker from the Justice Party. The whole incident shows what a big influence Druking had been unleashing.

5-7.
A SIGNIFICANT INCIDENT THAT MADE NAVER STOP EDITING NEWS STORIES

The Druking scandal was the final straw with regard to the controversy surrounding how Naver was manipulating the display of its news articles. On May 9, 2018, Naver announced the "News Service Improvement Plan."

Naver CEO Han Seong-sook announced that Naver will no longer edit and post news articles on the Naver homepage. And she also said she agrees to adopt the out-link system like Google, so that when users click certain news articles, they would be redirected to the websites of the news media that wrote the respective news articles. Her message was that, since Naver was implicated in the comment-rigging on the Naver news website, she was determined to separate it from the source. In this way, comments to news articles will be under the control of the news media outlets, instead of Naver.

Naver also decided to overhaul its controversial selective display of news stories from other news media outlets on its main page based on their opinion of their significance. The portal decided to use a new system

5. CURRENT STATUS OF THE KOREAN MEDIA

Comparison of Naver news site and Google main page.

in which news articles edited by the original news media outlets will be displayed on Naver.

For example, while in the past, news stories about President Moon Jae-in by MBC, Democratic Party of Korea by KBS and KCTU by Hankyoreh were collected and displayed side by side on the Naver homepage. Naver will now display news stories by those outlets separately in their own designated sections. In this way, Naver users have the choice to select a specific section to have access to headlines and other articles created by

급상승 검색어	DataLab. 급상승 트래킹 ›
1~10위	11~20위

1 신아영
2 조선일보 손녀
3 붉은달 푸른해
4 이서원
5 황후의 품격
6 마녀의 레시피
7 택배 파업
8 exid
9 싱스트리트
10 한세대학교

2018. 11. 22. 15:35:00 기준 (?)

Screenshot of Naver search words ranking

the news media outlet of their choice.

Naver also announced it will eliminate the practice of "ranking trending words" which is based on real-time search words. This ranking of real-time search words is something hard to find on Google, but with this practice, Naver gave the impression that it was showing users the trend of public opinion based on the ranking of search words. However, it was discovered that Moon Jae-in supporters could easily manipulate this ranking. For example, an absurd search word made it to second on the rank on November 15, 2017: We Love You Kim Jung-sook. It turned out that it was the First Lady Kim Jung-sook's 63rd birthday. On the Facebook community titled "People Who Build the World where People Live with Moon Jae-in" created by Moon Jae-in supporters, somebody posted an instruction to the community members to post "We love you Kim Jung-sook" all together at specific times. They decided to post that message

5. CURRENT STATUS OF THE KOREAN MEDIA

Search words ranking race between the Peace Olympics and the Pyongyang Olympics

at 10:00am, 12:00pm and 2:00pm Korea time, and in fact, the message made it to second in the rank at the time. It was truly a comical happening. But their atrocity did not end there.

Moon Jae-in supporters made the words "Peace Olympics" the number one search word on January 24, 2018. It was Moon Jae-in's 65th birthday. The word "Peace", Pyunghwa in Korean, was in reference to President Moon Jae-in's statement, "Let's make the Pyeongchang Winter Olympics an opportunity for peace for the South and the North." Since what happened on Kim Jung-sook's birthday left a negative impression on many people, this rigging of trending by the Moon supporters backfired as well: "Pyongyang Olympics," a phrase that countered the words "Peace Olympics" began to pop up on the portal website spontaneously and quickly made it to second on the rank of trending words. This was a cheeky counteraction that used the similar pronunciation between the two words of Pyongyang and Pyunghwa (peace), in Korean. It was a war of trending words in which the weapons were words that sounded similar but had different meanings. The "Pyongyang Olympics" had a sarcastic hidden message because some people found President Moon Jae-in's promotion of peace to be a servile attempt to please the North and thought he was dedicating the Pyeongchang Olympics to Pyongyang. This sarcasm was generated because all three words — Pyeongchang, Pyunghwa (peace), and Pyongyang — sound similar in Korean.

In the end, Naver announced that the portal was committed to solving the trending word controversy from the roots. But it remains to be seen if Naver will push forward with the overhaul considering the Korean people's obsession with ranking. For one thing, the second largest portal site, Daum, seems to have decided to keep the current practice of ranking trending words and editing news. We will have to wait and see if Naver will make the brave decision, because if Naver overhauls the current practice of ranking trending words, Naver will become comparatively less interesting than Daum.

5-8.

NAVER LABOR UNION JOINS NATIONAL COUNCIL OF TRADE UNIONS

It is very likely that the controversy over Naver's fairness will continue. A labor union was formed at Naver, and to our surprise, the Naver labor union joined the Korean Confederation of Trade Unions (KCTU) on April 2, 2018. That means, the employees of Naver became KCTU members. It was a first in the 19-year history of Naver, and Naver is the first among IT companies except for large or foreign corporations to form a labor union. Even though Naver is an IT-related company, its labor union was granted a membership to the chemical, textile and food division within KCTU, because Naver is the first IT company to join the KCTU. The current number of employees working for Naver including its headquarters and affiliates except for the branch in Japan is almost 4,000.

Naver employees' membership in KCTU is likely to have impact on other IT companies. Now that the employees of Korea's biggest portal site have become members of KCTU, many are understandably concerned about how to ensure fairness in their practice of editing and posting news stories, blogs, and website layouts. Their concerns will continue to remain real and valid because Naver is already above the press in Korea.

5-9.

PRESIDENTIAL CHIEF SECRETARY AND MBC CHIEF EDITOR WITH A DAUM BACKGROUND / DAUM

I've already mentioned that the Senior Secretary to the President for Public Communication Yoon Young-chan is the former Naver vice-president. The Moon Jae-in administration did not pick people with ties to Naver only. Even though Naver is learning towards the Left, as I previously mentioned, Daum is leaning to the Left slightly more than Naver. Take the Blue House's new media secretary Chung Hye-seung, for example. She is the former Kakao vice president. Chung joined Daum in 2008 after having been a reporter for Munhwa Ilbo, and as of 2017, Daum was taken over and merged with Kakao. Therefore, even though the portal site is named Daum, the name of the company is Kakao. Chung became the vice president of Kakao in January 2017, and after President Moon Jae-in took office, she was scouted to become the Blue House secretary. Her case testifies to the close relationship between Daum and the Moon Jae-in administration. Another interesting example is Park Seong-je, who was appointed MBC chief editor on June 18, 2018. As of today, the president of MBC is Choi Seung-ho, who is a former deputy commissioner of the KCTU-affiliated National Union of Media Workers, and Park Seong-je

5. CURRENT STATUS OF THE KOREAN MEDIA

Chung Hye-seung (l.) and Park Seong-je (r.). Sohn Suk-hee in the middle is the president of the JTBC news reporting division.

is also a former commissioner of the KCTU-affiliated National Union of Media Workers MBC headquarters. Interestingly enough, Park Seong-je is Chung Hye-seung's husband. The example of this couple is enough to raise concerns over how objective and fair MBC will be.

5-10.
APPOINTMENT OF KBS AND MBC PRESIDENTS AND THE NATIONAL UNION OF MEDIA WORKERS

In the KBS, the board of directors picks its president, while in the MBC, the Foundation for Broadcast Culture appoints its president. KBS has 11 members on its board of directors, with seven of them appointed by the ruling party, plus four by the opposition parties. The MBC's Foundation for Broadcast Culture has nine members on its board of directors, with six of them appointed by the ruling party, and three by the opposition parties. It is structured to allow the ruling party to have the final say when it comes to their president. One might think that KBS and MBC could easily turn into right-leaning broadcast companies if a right-wing political party becomes the ruling party. But that can never happen because both companies have NUM, which is under the umbrella of KCTU. When the president of Korea, whose term is five years, is changed, KBS and MBC presidents can also be changed at any time. But their colleagues are a different story, because they will have to work with them for 30 to 40 years. Where most colleagues are members of NUM, they have to be conscious of the union's whereabouts. The real problem would arise when a left-wing party becomes the ruling party. When this

5. CURRENT STATUS OF THE KOREAN MEDIA

KBS and MBC labor union strikes.

happens, their presidents are picked by the left-wing government, and with all employees being members of the left-wing union, both KBS and MBC get a free pass to the left-leaning broadcasting content. That is a really serious problem.

Even worse, when the majority of employees are leftists, they are empowered to replace members of the board of directors. Let me use MBC as an example. On May 9, 2017, Moon Jae-in was sworn in to office after winning the presidential election that was held seven months earlier than usual in the wake of the impeachment of President Park Geun-hye. For President Moon, the presidents of broadcasting companies who were appointed during the Park Geun-hye administration must have been nuisances. If they wanted to replace the president, they first had to change the Foundation for Broadcast Culture board of directors, but at the time, six directors were appointed by the former ruling party during the Park administration, and only three were appointed by the new ruling party. Under those circumstances, the NUM stepped in and helped Moon Jae-

A NUM member is on a strike in front of the church Kim Won-bae used to go.

in replace the MBC president. The union took advantage of the system in which each time a director appointed by the former ruling party resigns, he could be replaced by a new director appointed by the new ruling party. On September 8, 2017, Yoo Eui-seon who was appointed by the former ruling party resigned from the board. The reason was not clearly explained, but it was alleged that he was under pressure from many directions. With the resignation of Yoo Eui-seon, , the members of the board who were appointed by the former ruling party went from six to five, and by the new ruling party, from three to four.

An incident that happened on September 17 was a good example that showed how the NUM pressured a specific board director. It started when members of the NUM visited Kim Won-bae, a director appointed by the old ruling party. Kim Won-bae was an elder at the Jungchon Methodist Church in Daejeon, and he was attending a sacred Sunday morning service when he was visited by the NUM members. He was shocked. Then the NUM members hung a banner and started to chant, demanding his resignation. Park Young-tae, the pastor of the church, confronted them and told them that their protest was inappropriate in a

5. CURRENT STATUS OF THE KOREAN MEDIA

house of worship. Kim Won-bae resisted for a month before he caved in and submitted his resignation as of October 18. After his resignation, the members of the board who were appointed by the former ruling party went from five to four, and by the new ruling party, it went up to five from four. That meant the members appointed by the new ruling party became the majority on the board.

Now that they had more members from the new ruling party, the union immediately started a campaign to replace the MBC president. In the end, Kim Jang-gyum, who was appointed during the Park Geun-hye administration was dismissed, and Choi Seung-ho, a former vice commissioner of NUM, became the new MBC president on December 7.

The same thing happened in KBS as if following a script. Originally, the KBS board of directors had seven members by the old ruling party, and four by the new ruling party. NUM targeted Kim Kyung-min, a professor from Hanyang University, and Kang Kyu-hyung, a professor from Myungji University. The NUM members went to Hanyang and

Kim Jang-gyum is dismissed and replaced by Choi Seung-ho.

NUM members protest demanding the resignation of the KBS board member Kang Kyu-hyung.

Myungji, held up banners, and demanded they resign from their posts in KBS. Eventually, Kim Kyung-min resigned first on October 11, 2017. Professor Kim complained about the pressure he was under, because it was unfair and unacceptable for the NUM to come to the college campus and demand his resignation. In the end, the number of members appointed by the former ruling party went from seven to six, while the ones appointed by the new ruling party went up from four to five. Now, the NUM only need one more director to quit and make the ruling party the majority on the board. But another member, Kang Kyu-hyung, refused to resign despite the NUM's pressure.

Then the Moon administration took a different approach to get Kang Kyu-hyung removed. This time, it was the audit. The Board of Audit and Inspection sent a letter to the Korea Communications Commission asking that they dismiss Kang on November 24, 2017, accusing him of having used a corporate credit card for personal purchases. Kang had allegedly charged about $3,000 on a corporate card over a span of two years. The Board claimed that he couldn't explain the charges, either because it was possible that he used the card for his family, or it was used in

5. CURRENT STATUS OF THE KOREAN MEDIA

a restaurant close to his house, or he didn't remember who he had dined with. In the end, the Korea Communications Commission approved his dismissal on December 27, 2017. Now that Kang Kyu-hyung was gone, the number of directors appointed by the former ruling party went down from six to five, and by the new ruling party went up from five to six. That's how the new ruling party became the majority on the KBS board of directors.

KBS immediately started the procedure to replace the president. On January 22, 2018, KBS dismissed Ko Dae-young who was appointed during President Park Geun-hye's government, and replaced him with Yang Seung-dong on February 26. Yang Seung-dong is the former president of Employees Action, which was formerly a part of the NUM, and the chairman of the Producers Association.

Ultimately, KBS and MBC, the two largest broadcasting companies in Korea, were able to have leftist presidents who support the Moon Jae-in administration, and the string of campaigns was spearheaded by

Ko Dae-young is removed and replaced by Yang Seung-dong.

NUM. Now that the NUM and the Moon Jae-in's government joined forces to appoint their choices of KBS and MBC presidents, it is obvious which direction their reporting will take. Since KBS and MBC are not news-only broadcasting companies, it is clearly predictable what kind of political views they will reflect in dramas and variety shows.

5-11.
DEMOCRATIC PARTY OF KOREA ATTEMPTS TO OCCUPY THE BROADCASTING INDUSTRY

After becoming a ruling party, the Democratic Party of Korea had a workshop for their lawmakers at the Hongik University International Training Center, Jochiwon-eup, Sejong-si, on August 25, 2017. During this workshop, a document was distributed to the attendees, which was created at the Office of the Democratic Party Chief Counsels Office. The title of the document was "the Roadmap for the Normalization of Public Broadcasting." The "public broadcasting" consists of KBS and MBC. In reality, it was a document that detailed their plan to occupy the broadcasting industry. The specific action plan is as follows:

First, we will work together with members of broadcasting companies, citizen groups, and academics to carry out a campaign for the resignation of the presidents.

Second, we will investigate illegal activities of presidents such as corruption by using the supervising and managing power of the Korea Communications Commission.

Third, we will screen members of the board of directors who have ties

Democratic Party members in a workshop.

to the opposition party (the previous ruling party) and force them to resign by highlighting their corruption.

When the Democratic Party was in hot water after the content of the document was leaked, they defended themselves claiming that it was just a list of ideas from the staff in charge, but to my surprise, everything worked out according to their roadmap. It was beyond amazing. The NUM pulled off campaigns to dismiss the presidents, and the directors with ties to the previous ruling party were let go. And in due course, the presidents were replaced.

5-12.

SECRET INSPECTION AND RETALIATION IN MBC

On May 18, 2018, MBC fired announcer Choi Dae-hyun and reporter Kwon Ji-ho, because they were found to have created a blacklist, according to MBC. The MBC audit department might have wanted to punish them based on their own scenario, in which Choi Dae-hyun and Kwon Ji-ho made a blacklist on the instruction of the executives including president Kim Jang-gyum. But they could not find any evidence that corroborated the accusation that Choi Dae-hyun and Kwon Ji-ho made a blacklist on the instruction of the management. I want to bring your attention to the fact one more time: Even the MBC President Kim Jang-gyum, who was appointed during the Park Geun-hye administration, was not the man in power in MBC. The power was always in the hands of the NUM in MBC — it was in the past, and it is now. Choi Dae-hyun and Kwon Ji-ho confided that they were enraged at how the opportunists who belonged to the NUM and were fawning over the management were assigned to good posts. So they made the blacklist to record their true nature and make others aware of it. It was a record of the past whereabouts of rats, made with a sincere intention to identify hypocrites.

Announcer Choi Dae-hyun

If the act of making a blacklist itself is wrong, then I have a question. On December 14, 2016, the NUM announced the "list of journalist collaborators." My question is, isn't this truly a blacklist? On December 14, 2016, the NUM announced a list of ten reporters who they claimed have collaborated with the Lee Myung-bak and Park Geun-hye's governments, and went on to announce the names of an additional 50 journalists in April 2017, and 41 journalists in June the same year. There were 101 in total. Those were the people who had to be let go from KBS and MBC, according to their logic. The word "collaborator" has a seriously terrifying connotation in Korea. During the Korean War, the North Korean communists hunted down villagers who had supported the US or South Korea and executed them not with guns, but with bamboo spears, accusing them of being "collaborators" or "reactionaries." The NUM used the same abhorrent word to accuse and expose their own colleagues. The South Korea of the 21st century is swept up in the McCarthyism that seems to belong only in the 1950s. President Moon Jae-in himself is engaged in the act of "blacklist" retaliation under such slogans as "drive to end deep-

5. CURRENT STATUS OF THE KOREAN MEDIA

A list of journalists accused of being collaborators is released.

rooted corruption."

The problem is how and on what grounds did the MBC audit department claim to have found a blacklist made by Choi Dae-hyun and Kwon Ji-ho. The auditor presented emails to Choi Dae-hyun and Kwon Ji-ho as evidence. It is shocking and terrifying. Choi Dae-hyun and Kwon Ji-ho never gave anybody permission to access their emails. That means, the audit department had made an unauthorized search of the employee emails. The auditor, Park Young-choon, appeared at the Foundation for Broadcast Culture meeting on March 22, 2018 and confessed he had searched emails of 40 employees. If that's the number he admitted to, no doubt there are more that he did not admit. I filed a complaint over this unauthorized email search, and the case is in the prosecutor's office now. The Liberty Korea Party also filed a complaint with the prosecution on the same issue. The question is how committed the prosecution is to the case. We will just have to watch and see if the prosecution does what it is supposed to do under Moon Jae-in's government.

Auditor Park Young-choon

Six MBC employees including myself had to spend several months in a room that was used as for lighting storage. One of the six was Bae Hyun-jin, who had been an anchor of the MBC prime time news program News Desk for seven years. It was MBC President Choi Seung-ho's truly narrow-minded, pathetic retaliation: In my case, I must have been his target for having established a labor union at MBC, and for the MBC star anchor Bae Hyun-jin, she must have been targeted for having left NUM. In addition to the six who were moved to the lighting storage room, 80 more from the reporting desk had their microphones taken away. Interesting as it is, none of them were members of NUM. That's how Choi Seung-ho, a former executive of the NUM, bullies those who refuse to sign up.

That was not the end of his retaliation spree. He recalled all correspondents who were sent overseas when Kim Jang-gyum was the head of MBC. All those MBC correspondents who were sent to Washington DC, New York, Los Angeles, Paris, Bangkok, Beijing, and Tokyo had to suddenly pack and return to Korea. In truth, this is almost a human rights violation. In general, when you become a correspondent overseas,

5. CURRENT STATUS OF THE KOREAN MEDIA

Bae Hyun-jin (r.) and Kim Se-eui (l.) are testifying as victims.

you are guaranteed to have two years, and possibly a one-year extension to stay in the foreign city. Therefore, they should have been guaranteed to work from those cities for the minimum of two years. This term is important especially for their children's education. In the case of MBC correspondent to Tokyo, Kang Myung-il, he was notified to return home after just four months. It was truly a bolt out of the blue. It was not fair to his spouse who had to sign a lease for the house planning to live there for two years or more, and the children who had to transfer to schools in a foreign country just a few months ago.

On June 26, 2018, the MBC Chief Editor Park Sang-hoo was fired. Park was not a member of the NUM either. He was fired because he was wrong to criticize the surviving families of the Sewol ferry victims, and he was also wrong when he criticized Seoul Mayor Park Won-soon. They are truly absurd and ridiculous accusations. Isn't the press supposed to criticize with no bias or preference, and keep political power in check? Does that mean the surviving families of the ferry victims and the Seoul City Mayor Park Won-soon are exempt from criticism by the Korean press? It is outrageous that they judge and fire other journalists based on their own definition of "justice."

Then on July 4, 2018, Seoul Western District Prosecutor's Office reached a significant decision. In fact, I am surprised and grateful that the prosecution of the Moon Jae-in government made such a fair decision. I believe it proved that, after all, the prosecution is not just on the side of political power only. The Seoul Western District Prosecutor's Office announced that it decided to clear reporter Kwon Ji-ho on the complaint filed by Kwon Hyuk-yong, a member from the KCTU-affiliated NUM's MBC headquarters, accusing Kwon Ji-ho of having violated "the trade union and labor relations adjustment act." The prosecution stated, "It is difficult to prove that a document made by an ordinary reporter, Kwon Ji-ho, had somehow influenced the personnel changes in cameramen." This is just the beginning. Currently, many journalists including Kwon Ji-ho have filed lawsuits for unfair disciplinary action committed by MBC. Lawsuits against MBC President Choi Seung-ho's unfair dismissal of employees have now gone a step further. The "Notice of Reason for Dismissal and Disposition Not to Institute a Public Action" issued by the Seoul Western District Prosecutor's Office stated, "Even though it is confirmed

MBC President Choi Seung-ho

that the MBC audit team checked the emails of the suspects...(sic)... it is acknowledged that no evidence has been found to corroborate the claim that the accused had created the document at the instruction of their employer." This decision proved that the MBC audit team admittedly searched the emails of employees including Kwon Ji-ho. The prosecution must investigate the MBC audit team for their illegal search of e-mails of employees. In addition, strong punishment is due not just for the MBC audit team but also the MBC President, Choi Seung-ho.

6. EXAMPLES OF THE KOREAN PRESS SEIZED BY THE KOREA CONFEDERATION OF TRADE UNIONS

6-1.
OVERESTIMATED CANDLELIGHT RALLIES, UNDERESTIMATED TAEGUKGI RALLIES

On October 24, 2016, JTBC aired a report about "Choi Soon-sil and her tablet PC'. Then on March 10, 2017, the Constitutional Court decided to uphold the impeachment removing President Park Geun-hye from office. The impeachment of President Park Geun-hye was largely attributed to the candlelight protests. The candlelight rallies were orchestrated by a group called "People's Action for Immediate Resignation of President Park Geun-hye" which is an alliance of over 2,300 groups, mostly centering on KCTU, People's Solidarity for Participatory Democracy, People Uprising HQ, Baek Nam-gi Struggle HQ and other left-leaning citizen groups. The head of the People's Action for Immediate Resignation of President Park Geun-hye was Park Seok-woon, who also co-chaired the Coalition of Democratic Press and Citizens and the Legion of the Korean Progressive. Park Seok-woon is a man who appeared at the massive rally against the US beef imports that happened in 2008 as well. It is noteworthy that Park Seok-woon took the lead in the candlelight rally that had effectively dealt a serious a blow to the Lee Myung-bak administration soon after his inauguration by creating the "mad cow disease scare" associated with the US beef imports, and this time, he did the same to the Park Geun-hye administration with the help of candlelight rallies.

KBS, MBC, and numerous other broadcasting channels reported the candlelight rallies as major feature stories. Among them, SBS, in particular, was more passionate than others as if it was competing with JTBC.

SBS is a broadcasting company founded by Yoon Se-young, the chairman of Taeyoung Group whose main business is construction. Unlike KBS and MBC, SBS is a privately-owned broadcasting company, and it has an interesting group of employees. While KBS and MBC have the NUM headquarters and their own labor unions, SBS has only the NUM headquarters. That means, SBS is fully exposed to the rule of NUM without any countering union.

There were 20 candlelight rallies beginning on October 29, 2016 and ending on March 11, which is the day after the Constitutional Court upheld the decision to impeach President Park Geun-hye on March 10, 2017. SBS started live television broadcast of candlelight rallies on Gwanghwamun Square every week starting on November 5, 2016. On February 4, 2017, SBS reporters were covering stories about the day's candlelight rally on live tv during their prime-time news program Eight O'clock News. However, there were not too many people who came to the rally on this particular day. Despite the scanty protesters that viewers could see on the TV screen, the news program had a subtitle on the screen that read: "a large crowd came to the square for the first candlelight rally since last week." It could have been just an accident resulting from an ill-prepared live broadcast, but the scene and the subtitle did not match at all. They should never have used that kind of subtitle if the majority of the protesters had already left the square and were marching in the direction of the Blue House. I believe there are a lot of news media

A screenshot of the SBS news report dated February 4, 2017. The news reported it was a large crowd, but the photo tells it was not.

outlets including SBS that need to reflect on themselves and ask if they were not too carried away with regard to their coverage of the candlelight rallies.

It was on November 19, 2016 that the first so-called "Taegukgi Rallies" started happening to counter the candlelight rallies. The first Taegukgi rally took place at the Seoul Station Square, which was about 4km away from the Gwanghwamun Square where a candlelight rally was taking place, and they were mostly members from about 80 right-wing groups including "Legion of Park Geun-hye Supporters." According to the organizers, there were about 67,000 people who came to the rally, and according to the police, the number was about 11,000. Major broadcasting companies such as KBS, MBC, and SBS covered the stories about the rally on their main news programs. KBS had eleven news stories about the candlelight rally, and just one about the Taegukgi rally, while MBC had nine news stories about the candlelight rally, and just one about the Taegukgi rally.

The problem was SBS, whose coverage was truly ill-intended no mat-

6. EXAMPLES OF THE KOREAN PRESS SEIZED BY THE KOREA CONFEDERATION OF TRADE UNIONS

ter how I look at it. First of all, SBS had over 25 news stories about the candlelight rally, but less than 0.5 about the Taegukgi rally. It was less than 0.5 because the story about the Taegukgi rally was part of a story about both the Taegukgi and candlelight rallies. But the worst part was the content of their coverage. I will explain later in further detail, but SBS did not follow the rule about the number of participants. While KBS and MBC reported the number of participating protesters based on estimates of both the rally organizers and police, SBS reported the number of candlelight protesters only based on information from rally organizers, and the number of Taegukgi protesters only based on the police figures, thereby attempting to inflate the size of the candlelight rally and understate the size of the Taegukgi rally. It was SBS reporter Chung Hye-kyung who covered the candlelight rally story live from Gwanghwamun Square, and she even went one step further to make a comment that denigrated the Taegukgi protesters. She reported,

"About 11,000 pro-Park Geun-hye supporters had a so-called counter demonstration to protest the impeachment of President Park Geun-hye at the Seoul Station Square beginning at 2:00pm today. These are members of about 70 pro-Park groups that we can't really call conservatives, and they chanted 'No to the impeachment of the President, yes to the protection of the Constitution.'"

She referred to the Taegukgi protesters as "members of pro-Park groups," making it sound like they were from President Park Geun-hye fan clubs. She made a denigrating comment about the Taegukgi protesters by saying "pro-Park groups that we can't really call conservatives." The SBS reporter made a particular point of quoting candlelight rally organizers when she said about 750,000 protesters joined the candlelight rally but did not mention anything about the estimate by the police which was 180,000. On the other hand, she quoted only the police when she said the Taegukgi rally had 11,000 protesters but made no mention about the estimate of the organizers which was about 67,000. This kind of reporting can only be described as malicious.

Beginning on November 19, the Taegukgi rally happened every Saturday just as the candlelight rallies did. But none of the news media demonstrated any sense of balance in their coverage of them. On November 26, KBS covered the candlelight rally in 15 stories, but only one story about the Taegukgi rally; MBC had 14 stories about the candlelight rally, but one about the Taegukgi rally; and SBS had 37 stories about the candlelight rally, but none about the Taegukgi rally. On December 3, KBS had 9 stories about the candlelight rally, and one about the Taegukgi rally; MBC had 12 about the candlelight rally, and one about the Taegukgi rally; SBS had 23 about the candlelight rally, and one about the Taegukgi rally. KBS and MBC definitely had issues with unbalanced coverage of the rallies, but SBS was the worst.

Then something happened that shocked everyone on January 7, 2017: It was the day when the Taegukgi rally figures outnumbered the candlelight rally. It was estimated that 1.02 million participated in the Taegukgi rally according to its organizers, or 37,000 according to the police. The candlelight rally had only about 600,000 according to its organizers, or 24,000 according to the police. Then the protesters who came to the rally to demand the impeachment of President Park Geun-hye started criticizing the police. They claimed the police intentionally underestimated the number of candlelight protesters and significantly overestimated that of the Taegukgi protesters. As the controversy over the number kept growing, the police decided not to announce their estimate of protesters as of January 14. With this decision, Koreans became stripped of their opportunity to get an objective estimate of the numbers of protesters, be it the candlelight rally or the Taegukgi rally.

On March 1st, Independence Movement Day, which was a few days before the Constitutional Court was to announce a decision on the impeachment case, an enormous number of people came to the Taegukgi rally. It was difficult to figure out just how many people came after the police had decided not to announce their own estimate of protesters, but the Taegukgi rally clearly outnumbered the candlelight rally by far. The organizers of the Taegukgi rally estimated it to be 5 million, while the candlelight organizers claimed the number was just about 300,000.

On the day when the Taegukgi rally significantly outnumbered the candlelight rally, the SBS 8 O'clock News anchor Kim Seong-joon told the co-anchor Kim Jong-won, "Those who supported the impeachment came mostly with their families, while everybody who came to rally to protest against it came in a rain poncho, as if somebody had distributed it to them."

This comment can be also called malicious, because he made it look like the pro-impeachment protesters came voluntarily with their families, while the anti-impeachment protesters were mobilized on an organizational level because they were in rain ponchos that seemed to have been distributed to them.

6-2.

ABOLISHMENT OF THE RULE ABOUT ESTIMATES BOTH BY THE ORGANIZERS AND THE POLICE

The policy on reporting rally participant numbers was abolished during the "candlelight conjuncture." The objectivity of the Korean press was lost in the aftermath of the controversy over the number of protesters. In principle, the press has to report the number of protesters estimated by both the rally organizers and the police. That is the rule all reporters whose beat is social affairs have to follow. Let me give you a few examples.

On November 19, 2016, there was a candlelight rally by those who demanded that President Park Geun-hye resign. The organizers estimated 600,000 people came to the rally, while the police estimated it was more like 180,000, not quite a third of the organizers' figure. KBS and MBC followed the rule and reported numbers by the organizers and the police. But SBS reported the estimate by the organizers only, and none by the police. SBS went one step further when it reported that the number of candlelight protesters was 750,000 if the number of people who came from around the country was included, as claimed by the organizers.

People kept raising questions about the credibility of the organizers' claim, but it seemed the Korean news media outlets, particularly SBS, had no issue with it. So let's see how they did with other rallies.

On November 12, 2016, the organizers claimed one million, and the police, 260,000, which is nearly four times the figure. On November 26, the difference was five times with the organizers claiming 1.3 million, and the police claiming 260,000. The organizers seemed to be getting more audacious. On December 3, the organizers said it was 1.6 million, while the police said it was 250,000, making the difference 6.4 times. The difference was 5.9 times on December 10 with the organizers claiming 600,000 and the police, 102,000, and then the difference was ten times on December 17 with the organizers claiming 600,000 and the police, 60,000.

It didn't end there. The difference was a whopping 16.7 times on December 24 when the organizers claimed it was 600,000 but the police claimed it was only 36,000.

Given the situation, any right-minded reporters would naturally raise questions about the numbers the organizers were claiming. But the press kept focusing only on the estimates claimed by the candlelight rally

The difference between the estimates by the organizers and the police was a whopping 16.7 times.

organizers. Eventually, on January 1, 2017, the press reported that the number of protesters at the candlelight rally had reached 10 million, and made it sound as if almost all Koreans were supporting the impeachment of President Park Geun-hye. Newsis covered the story on January 1, 2017 under a headline that read, "President Park's Impeachment-Demanding Candlelight Protesters Reach 10 Million – a New History of Demonstration is Written." It was only a number claimed by the organizers of the candlelight rally, but Newsis made an emotional report as if it was a historic fact. Newsis was not alone — the situation was the same throughout the news media.

According to the Ministry of Government Administration and Home Affairs, the population of Korea as of May 2018 was 51,790,000. Candlelight rally organizers claimed that from the first candlelight rally on October 29, 2016 to its tenth on December 31, ten million people participated in the rallies. Can we really believe that one fifth of the entire country came to rally in such a short span of time? Besides, Gwanghwamun Square in Jongno-gu, Seoul, is 18,840 m^2. Of course, the size of the venue can stretch if Cheonggye Square and Seoul City Hall Square are included. But no matter how far you stretch, it cannot be bigger than 200,000 m^2. Given that, anybody could see that accidents were inevitable if millions gathered in that size of a venue. But the Korean media ignored the possibility and kept itself busy writing down the announcement of the rally organizers.

Practically having her executive power been suspended already, President Park Geun-hye's government was being dragged by the Korean press forces behind the candlelight rallies, and the Democratic Party of Korea. The police decided not to announce its estimate of the number of protesters as of January 14, 2017. It was a day when the police lost one of its main functions. As I mentioned previously, the difference in the estimated number of protesters was a staggering 16.7 times between the organizers and the police, which were 600,000 and 36,000 respectively. Even though the police were supposed to give an accurate account of this vast difference, it caved in to pressure from the candlelight protesters and voluntarily gave up that duty.

6-3.

THE PRESS PULLS EVEN THE US EMBASSY IN SEOUL INTO THE CANDLELIGHT RALLY

During the candlelight rally that took place on December 3, 2016, the protesters observed one minute of darkness in an event came to be known as "one-minute of lights-out." The next day, many news media outlets including Yonhap News Agency started spewing out ridiculous reports, most of which centered around the same claim: The US Embassy

A screenshot of the Kukmin Ilbo article.

6. EXAMPLES OF THE KOREAN PRESS SEIZED BY THE KOREA CONFEDERATION OF TRADE UNIONS

Lawmaker Lee Yong-ju claimed the US Embassy had participated in the one-minute lights-out event.

in Korea was caught having participated in the "one-minute lights-out" event. It was only gossip talked about by online users, but the press made irresponsible reports about it without bothering to check the facts. Kukmin Ilbo even made it sound like a confirmed fact by printing an article on December 4, 2016 under a title that read "Even the US Embassy to Korea Joins the One-minute Lights-Out."

The whole episode shows how irresponsible the Korean press is. As if that was not enough, Lee Yong-ju, the then-lawmaker from the People's Party, presented a blown-up photo that showed how the lights seemed to have been turned off at the US Embassy building during the parliamentary investigation of the political scandal that involved Choi Soon-sil that happened at the National Assembly on December 5, and said it seemed the US Embassy was participating in the one-minute lights-out event that happened during the candlelight rally. It testified to the sub-standard reality of not just the Korean press, but also the Korean parliament. The US Embassy spokesperson made a statement denying it, saying, "The lights at the Embassy stayed on," and their official position on the issue was that "we did not participate in the one-minute lights-out event." The US Ambassador to Korea Mark Lippert repeated it again when he met the press on the 9th. He said, "The US Embassy in Korea does not get involved in the domestic politics of South Korea."

6-4.

HUMAN RIGHTS ISSUES IN NORTH KOREA BEING IGNORED BY THE SOUTH KOREAN PRESS

Hankook Ilbo printed a truly shameful article on June 8, 2018. The title of the article was "Peace in the Korean Peninsula is More Important than Human Rights in North Korea." I could not believe what I was looking at. I wondered if it was the title of a post by a blogger, but it was not. It was clearly the title of a Hankook Ilbo article. It was not just an

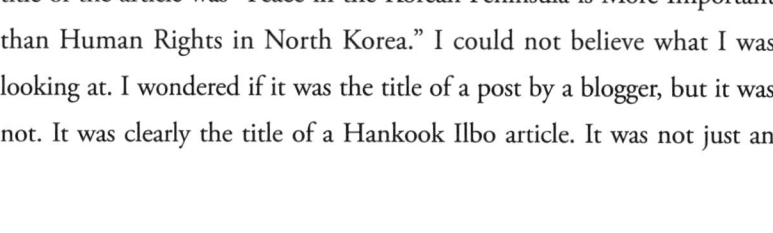

A shocking Hankook Ilbo article printed on the top of a page on June 9, 2018.

article available in the online edition either: It was the headline printed on the top of page 26 dated June 9, 2018. The article was written by Ko Jae-ha, a Hankook Ilbo editor, which means he was a senior reporter, not a junior reporter. I could not help but question his intent in writing such an absurd article and printing it. The content of the article was more shocking.

It read:
"Human rights in North Korea is an issue that polarizes South Korea. Conservative groups are persistently demanding that Moon Jae-in's government and US President Donald Trump make the issue an agenda item."
"Even though human rights is a universal value, we cannot completely disregard the regional characteristics of each country, such as their history, culture, and religion."
"Human rights in North Korea is not just a North Korean issue. It can easily escalate into argument over its universality and distinct characteristics, unless it is explained in connection with the end of the system divided into the North and the South."

It is a truly hard-to-understand point, and it took me quite a while to understand it. The basics of writing an article is that you have to write it so that it's easy and convenient for the reader to understand. In short, Ko's point can be explained as "we need to forget about the suffering of the North Koreans for the sake of peace in the Korean Peninsula, because making human rights in the North an issue can result in heightened tension in the Korean peninsula." I don't know if Ko Jae-hak is a leftist, but one of the special characteristics of leftists is that they tend to make a simple point sound a lot more complicated. I'm not sure exactly why, but I believe it is because they are afraid that their poor logic might be exposed if they speak simply and clearly. In Korea, there is a saying that's been around for some time now: "The talkative ones are the communists." That's what comes from people who were personally victimized by communists during the Korean War. That means communists enjoy deceiving people with complicated explanations instead of clear and simple explanations.

Let's go back to the article by Ko Jae-hak. He claimed, "Human rights in North Korea is an issue that polarizes South Korea." When he said "polarizes," he means the conflict between the Left and the Right within South Korea. As pointed out by Ko Jae-hak, the leftists in South Korea find it uncomfortable to bring up the issue regarding human rights in North Korea, because they believe the issue is a stumbling block for peace in the Korean Peninsula. It is a cowardly mindset that tells us how they care only about their political cause and security. I believe it is more than just cowardly: I think it is evil.

I doubt Ko Jae-hak's article came out of nowhere. The left-wing has always claimed the same. Let's take the statement made by Moon Chung-in, who is President Moon Jae-in's close aide and whose name is even similar to the President. Moon Chung-in is a special advisor to President Moon Jae-in for foreign affairs and national security. At a current affairs speech event that happened at Ewha Womans University on June 14, 2018, he argued, "We should not use the human rights issue as a prerequisite of our negotiations with the North," because, according to him, "denuclearization is what matters most at the moment." He continued, "President Moon Jae-in brought up the human rights issues to the North, but he didn't prioritize it. Building trust between the South and the

North is a bigger priority than the human rights issue." This statement made by President Moon Jae-in's closest aide, Moon Chung-in, seemed to march along with the position of the Korean press.

If I may talk about Moon Chung-in briefly, he is an anti-American political figure who had supported the withdrawal of USFK numerous times and who held a negative opinion about the Korea-US alliance. It is hard to figure out where his strong anti-American sentiment comes from considering his ties to America: He got his MA and Ph.D. degrees in political science from Maryland University in the US; he was an associate professor of political science at the University of Kentucky; and he was an adjunct professor at Duke University Asia-Pacific Studies Institute.

In an interview with the American current affairs magazine the *Atlantic* on May 17, 2018, he said he wanted the Korea-US alliance to end, because alliances in general are a "very unnatural state of international relations." He went on to say that for him, the best thing was to really "get rid of" the alliance. In the column he contributed to the *Foreign Affairs* dated April 30, 2018, he claimed that when a peace treaty is signed between the South and the North, "it will be difficult to justify the US forces' continuing presence in South Korea." These are claims that we cannot brush off as the radical opinion of an individual, because, as the special advisor for the president on unification, diplomacy, and national security, he has been sharing the majority of his ideas on affairs regarding the Korean Peninsula with President Moon Jae-in since President Moon was a presidential candidate. In his keynote address at a seminar in Washington DC hosted by the East Asia Foundation and the Woodrow Wilson International Center for Scholars on June 16, 2017, Moon Chung-in argued, "Seoul may discuss reducing US strategic asset deployment and downscaling joint military exercises with Washington if Pyongyang halts its nuclear and missile activities." Responding to the growing controversy caused by his remarks, Moon defended himself claiming that it was just a personal remark he'd made as a professor. But Moon Chung-in's remark turned into reality a year later: On June 19, 2018, the Korean and US governments decided to temporarily suspend the UFG (Ulchi-Freedom Guardian) military exercise. If Moon Chung-in had indeed revealed the intention of President Moon Jae-in at the seminar, it seems the withdrawal of 28,000 US soldiers who are serving in South Korea to ensure the security of the Korean Peninsula will become a reality sooner, rather than later.

Let's go back to human rights in North Korea. North Korea being one of the most secluded regimes, nobody can tell with certainty, but it is estimated that in the North, there are six political prison camps where 154,000 prisoners are locked up, including not just "traitors" and "reactionaries" but also their families including little children as young as six years old who are put to 12 hours of heavy labor, according to testimony.

Those who have the audacity to claim that human rights in the North can wait for the sake of the peace in the Korean Peninsula will soon have to face the accusation of being devils who have relinquished the dignity of being humans.

According to a report by the Voice of America on June 30, 2018, Christopher Smith, a Republican lawmaker and a member of the House Foreign Affairs Committee, claimed "Improvement of human rights in North Korea has to be included in the strategy to denuclearize the Korean Peninsula." In this resolution, Christopher Smith also said, "Improvement of human rights in North Korea that is fully verifiable and irrevocable has to be part of the strategy for a free and open Indo-Pacific region."

In the 2018 Trafficking in Persons Report Launch Ceremony that took place on June 28, 2018, US Secretary of State Mike Pompeo identified North Korea as one of the examples of human trafficking and described it as "tragic." In fact, North Korea has been identified as "the worst example of human trafficking" for 16 years straight since 2003. Given that, I cannot understand why the human rights issue in North Korea is not the priority for the Moon Jae-in administration in South Korea. The left-wing camp has been praising the North as being the same nation and advocated anti-America and anti-Japan strategies, but why are they ignoring the suffering of North Koreans who they claim are their fellow Koreans? Don't they feel ashamed that America is more concerned about North Koreans who are the same people as us? It makes me shudder when I think about the leftists' hypocrisy.

6-5.

OVEREXTENDED PRAISE OF KIM JONG-UN

President Moon Jae-in and North Korean leader Kim Jong-un had an inter-Korean summit in Panmunjom on April 27, 2018. Soon after, the Korean press began churning out articles that praised not just President Moon Jae-in, but also the North's leader Kim Jong-un.

On April 30, 2018 on its prime-time news program 8 O'clock News, MBC reported "Seven out of every eight Koreans in the South trust Kim Jong-un," quoting the results of a telephone survey of 1,023 men and women over the ages of 19 by Korea Research Center that specializes in polls. According to the report, 60.5% of respondents answered they "mostly trust" what Kim Jong-un said and did during the summit, and 17.1% answered they "absolutely trust." When those who answered "mostly" or "absolutely" trusted Kim are combined, a whopping 77.5% of the respondents turned out to trust him.

On the prime-time news program 9 O'clock News on the same day, KBS also reported "80% of Koreans in the South have become more positive in their trust of Kim Jong-un." KBS reported that it was the result of a poll about "how their perception of Kim Jong-un had changed after the South-North Summit that was aired live for 12 hours." According to KBS, 22.3% of respondents answered it changed to "very positive" and 57.7% answered it changed to "relatively positive." When combined, as much as 80% of the respondents answered that their perception was changed to positive. These were the results of an online survey of 1,077 Korean men and women over the age of 19 around the country for a day, on April 30 by KBS Broadcast Research Institute.

As the poll by KBS shows, the South-North Summit that the Korean news media outlets aired live for 12 hours on April 27, 2018 completely changed people's perception of the North Korean leader Kim Jong-un. It testified to the power of Korean broadcasting companies.

If you take a look into the reports the broadcasting companies aired on April 27, there is no wonder people began to favor him. KBS reporter Shin Bang-sil described Kim Jong-un as being candid and daring in her coverage under the title "Unconventional, Candid, Daring 'Kim Jong-un Style'…. His Every Move Attracts Attention."

MBC had two reporters cover stories about Kim Jong-un. MBC reporter Lee Nam-ho's coverage had the title "Kim Jong-un Style – Daring, Candid, Manners, Nervous'" and MBC reporter Lim Myung-chan's coverage had the title "Kim Jong-un Chooses the Formal Mao Jacket — Is the Dress a Message?" Introducing these stories, anchor Park Seong-ho said, "The Kim Jong-un I saw today was a man with a sense of humor, relaxed, and candid." I wonder, based on what did the anchor Park Seong-ho judge Kim Jong-un to be a candid man.

SBS reporter Kim Soo-hyung had coverage titled "Nervous, Relaxed, Daring, Kim Continues to Surprise – His Global Debut." With KBS, MBC, and SBS competitively presenting coverage that was in favor of

Kim Jong-un, there is no wonder that people's perception of Kim Jong-un became favorable.

Uriminzokkiri, a North Korean state-controlled website that is used for propaganda to the South, reported that "Kim Jong-un" fever was heating up in South Korea. The website also had a story that described how Kim Jong-un had "captivated the people in the South by showing them he is a confident and open-minded international leader." It is deplorable that even the North Korean media reported how the South was jumping on the bandwagon of Kim Jong-un praise.

6-6.
NORTH KOREA PRAISE IN FULL SWING BEGINNING WITH THE PYEONGCHANG OLYMPICS

Previously, I talked about how the search terms "Peace Olympics" and "Pyeongchang Olympics" were in a race to become number one on the portal Naver's list of real-time hot trending words on President Moon's birthday, January 24, 2018, shortly before the opening of the Pyeongchang Olympics.

Numerous Korean corporations and the Gangwon Province government worked hard to bring the winter Olympics to Pyeongchang. Korea had tried its luck to host the 2010 winter Olympics at the IOC session that happened in Prague, Czech in July 2003, only to be defeated by Vancouver, Canada.

I had the opportunity to witness the second bid to host the winter Olympics in Pyeongchang. It was at the IOC session that took place in Guatemala City in Guatemala in July 2007. Pyeongchang had fierce competition from a few other cities the second time around to host the 2014 winter Olympics, and I was left in tears when Pyeongchang lost the bid again, this time to Sochi, Russia.

There were people who said it was time to give up, but Pyeongchang

6. EXAMPLES OF THE KOREAN PRESS SEIZED BY THE KOREA CONFEDERATION OF TRADE UNIONS

didn't. In July 2011, Pyeongchang defeated München of Germany and Annecy of France at the IOC session that took place in Durban, South Africa, and finally, Pyeongchang was announced as the host city of the 2018 Winter Olympics. The feat was credited to the hard work of President Lee Myung-bak, Korean Air chairman Cho Yang-ho, Doosan Group Chairman Park Yong-sung, and Samsung Chairman Lee Kun-hee and many others who did not give up.

It was indeed a splendid feat that came after tremendous effort by many people. The residents of Pyeongchang, Gangwon Province, anticipated that the Olympics would bring them an opportunity to grow the region that was falling behind other regions. But President Moon Jae-in used the Pyeongchang Winter Olympics as an opportunity for him to develop more amicable relationship with Pyongyang on May 9, 2017. As a result, the people who were sent by the North Korean dictatorship regime stole all the limelight in Korea as well as in the world, and Pyeongchang, the city in Gangwon Province, was pushed away from center stage. As shown in the trending word controversy that happened on January 24 on the Naver portal site, Pyeongchang Olympics was no longer in the hearts of the Moon Jae-in supporters, and the "Peace Olympics" seemed to be all that mattered to them. In response to the Moon supporters, those who criticized Moon Jae-in countered with their own search term: Pyongyang Olympics. Consequently, Pyeongchang itself fell out of the spotlight due to the "Peace Olympics" that the Moon Jae-in administration and his supporters advocated.

6-7.
LUDICROUS FASCINATION WITH KIM YO-JONG

North Korea issued notice on February 7, 2018 that they were sending Kim Jong-un's sister Kim Yo-jong to South Korea as a part of a group of high-level North Korean delegates to the Pyeongchang Winter Olympics. Kim Jong-un's sister Kim Yo-jong is a figure blacklisted by The U.S. Treasury Department on January 11, 2018. But the Korean media reported her visit as if they were giving her an open-arm welcome under such headlines as follows:

KBS 'North Sends Surprise Delegate Kim Yo-jong'… The First Visit from the Mount Baekdu Bloodline (by Lim Jong-bin)

MBC 'Kim Yo-jong is Coming to the Olympics Opening'… The First Visit from the Mount Baekdu Bloodline (by Lee Yong-joo)

SBS 'Kim Jong-un's Sister Kim Yo-jong Coming to Pyeongchang'… First from the Mount Baekdu Bloodline to Visit South (by Kim Yong-tae)

All three national network channels – KBS, MBC, and SBS reported

Kim Yo-jong's visit to the South as a headline using such disgraceful terms as "Mount Baekdu Bloodline." As a Korean journalist, it was a humiliating day. The term "Mount Baekdu Bloodline" was used by Kim Jong-un's father Kim Jong-il to deify the direct family members of Kim Il-sung, such as Kim Jong-il, Kim Jong-un and Kim Yo-jong. It was so named because the founder of the North Korean regime Kim Il-sung was allegedly born with the energy of Mount Baekdu. Of course, Kim Jong-il's first son Kim Jong-nam and the second son Kim Jong-chul are also members of the Mount Baekdu Bloodline. But Kim Jong-nam, a member of the sacred and important Mount Baekdu Bloodline, was assassinated at Kuala Lumpur international airport in Malaysia on February 13, 2017 by having a lethal chemical called VX nerve agent forcefully smeared on his face and eyes by several women from Indonesia and Vietnam.

The US government did not make any official statement on the event, but the London-based international news agency Reuters reported there were many in the US government who believe Kim Jong-un was behind the assassination of Kim Jong-nam. The on-going investigation kept discovering more details that point fingers at Kim Jong-un as the man behind the assassination. On February 2017, Malaysia's police chief, Khalid Abu Bakar, said in a press conference that Hyun Gwang-seong, a senior diplomat at the North Korean Embassy, and Kim Wook-il, an employee of the North Korean state-owned airline, Air Koryo, were also wanted for questioning in connection with the assassination of Kim Jong-nam.

This case is just one example that shows how the term "Mount Baekdu Bloodline" is a disgrace in itself. But the Korean media shamelessly kept praising Kim Yo-jong, referring to her as a member of the Mount Baekdu Bloodline. What a comedy it is to revere somebody for being a member of a certain "bloodline" especially in this 21st century. In the case of the American TV series Game of Thrones, it sounds beautiful that one of the leading actors Jon Snow is supposedly from the noble bloodlines of the Targary and the Stark, but it's only because it is a fantasy story. With the case of the North Korean dictatorship, however, I have no other word except disgusted to describe how I feel about people revering Kim Il-sung, Kim Jong-il and Kim Jong-un, calling them members of the "Mount Baekdu Bloodline."

The historic Pyeongchang Winter Olympics opened in Korea on February 9, 2018. It was a festival of global sports fans that happened in Korea for the first time in 30 years after the Seoul Summer Olympics that began on September 17, 1988. But on this particular day, all the Korean news media outlets could not get enough coverage of Kim Jong-un's sister Kim Yo-jong who visited South Korea. It was pathetic that the Korean press cared so much about Kim Jong-un's sister. Yonhap News Agency, which wires news stories to media outlets throughout the country had an article on February 9 that read as follows:

"Kim Yo-jong, the sister of the Leader of the Workers' Party of Korea Kim Jong-un and Vice Director of the Propaganda and Agitation Department of the Workers' Party of Korea, channeled a classy and elegant style as she visits the South on the 9th to celebrate the 2018 Pyeongchang Winter Olympics."
"Kim Yo-jong's high-class fashion has a thread of connection with Hyun Song-wol, the leader of the Samjiyon Orchestra."

I know we should not judge people based on their looks. But once the subject came up, I cannot help myself wondering: Did they really think Kim Yo-jong looked elegant? On what basis were they judging her to be classy? Or were they just carried away while trying to praise her?

The articles also mentioned the fashion of Hyun Song-wol, the leader of the North's Samjiyon Orchestra. There is something about this subject that needs to be addressed too. Hyun Song-wol came to the South on January 22, 2018 to inspect the venue where the North Korean group of entertainers were to perform. The Korean press started praising Hyun Song-wol beginning from her very first visit as if they were competing with each other. Kim Yo-jong being Kim Jong-un's sister, the zeal may be understandable, but I cannot wrap my head around the zeal of the Korean press over Hyun Song-wol. Yonhap News Agency wired an article that day with the following headline:

Hyun Song-wol, Long coat, Fur, Ankle Boots …'Unassuming Yet Posh Looks' (by Kim Eun-kyung)

I don't know if South Korea is poor and substandard in terms of fashion, but it is pathetic that the press described Hyun Song-wol from the North as being "posh." On that day, Hyun Song-wol was wearing a fox scarf around her neck and carried a crocodile leather clutch by Hermes, a French luxury brand bag that costs over $22,000. When Hyun Song-wol showed up in expensive brand items, wasn't the Korean press supposed to criticize her instead of praising her? Hyun Song-wol is not a business woman. She is an entertainer who performs for the North's dictator Kim Jong-un. Given that, where would the money come from? Likewise, there is no doubt the wool coat that Kim Jong-un's sister Kim Yo-jong wore was just as expensive. As we are all aware, there are people dying of starvation in the North. Under those circumstances, is the Korean press justified in praising their posh taste in fashion?

According to a report by Daily NK on June 28, 2018, Kim Jong-un ordered the execution of a high-ranking North Korean army officer, accusing him of having rationed more food and fuel to the North Korean soldiers and their families.

The executed officer was Hyun Joo-sung, a high-ranking officer equivalent to lieutenant general in the North Korean army and in charge of inspection at the military supply department under the Ministry of the People's Armed Forces. He was reportedly hit by 90 bullets from nine shooters. The execution itself was gruesome, but it is terrifying how a man's life can be taken away by just one word from Kim Jong-un.

It is deplorable when I think about how long the Korean press will keep praising people who are close to the dictator Kim Jong-un, such as those who came from the North flashing a fox fur scarf, wool coat, and Hermes clutch as people in the North are suffering and dying of starvation.

6-8.
THE PRESS BECOMES THE SPOKESPERSONS FOR THE NORTH ABOUT THE CHEONAN SINKING INCIDENT

It was March 26, 2010 at 9:22 at night that the Cheonan, a corvette of the Republic of Korea Navy, was attacked by a torpedo near Baengnyeong Island in the West Sea, killing 46. Only 58 out of the 104 personnel onboard were rescued. On March 30, ROK Navy's Underwater Demolition Team (UDT) warrant officer, Han Ju-ho, lost consciousness while searching for survivors and was rushed to the hospital, but he died

Part of the Cheonan is recovered from the sea.

soon after. On April 4, the families of the victims held a press conference and asked that they stop the rescue operation because they did not want anybody to lose their lives while searching for survivors. It was a truly heart-breaking decision.

A joint civilian-military investigation group was created to discover the cause of the incident that came to be known as the "Cheonan Sinking." It was a large investigative team of 74 that included 25 from various institutions in Korea, 22 from the military, three recommended by the National Assembly, and 24 from four countries including the US, Australia, Great Britain and Sweden. The joint investigative team announced its official conclusion, saying, "A North Korean torpedo sank the ship Cheonan," and that "a non-contact underwater explosion" was the cause of the sinking. According to the investigation, "the North Korean torpedo was detonated three meters to port from the center of the gas turbine room and at a depth of 6-9 meters," and "the Cheonan was split and sunk due to a shockwave and bubble effect generated by the underwater explosion of the torpedo."

The torpedo part clearly marked "number 1" in Korean.

6. EXAMPLES OF THE KOREAN PRESS SEIZED BY THE KOREA CONFEDERATION OF TRADE UNIONS

A screenshot of the article about official apology from OhmyNews.

The joint investigative team also made public the torpedo parts recovered at the site of the explosion, which included markings clearly written in Korean with blue ink "number 1" inside the end of the propulsion section. The team explained that it was consistent with the North's practice of leaving handwritten marks on supply parts, such as the case of another North Korean torpedo discovered in 2003 with a marking that read "number 4" in Korean inside of it.

But the left-leaning Korean press refused to accept the conclusion about the North Korean torpedo. They turned to numerous experts and raised suspicion about the conclusion, questioning "how can the markings of 'number one' remain so clear?" or claiming, "the white residue found on the torpedo and the ship might be just rust left by a natural weathering process instead of evidence of explosion." Hankyoreh, Kyunghyang and OhmyNews were particularly skeptical about the North Korean torpedo theory. OhmyNews even claimed in its article dated March

A poster of the documentary movie, Cheonan Project.

24, 2011 that the red material found in the torpedo was red-colored sea squirt found not in the West Sea but in the East Sea. But when it was tested by the National Fisheries Research & Development Institute at the request of the Ministry of Defense, it turned out that the material was not a red sea squirt, and in fact, it was not even a living organism. Soon after, OhmyNews officially apologized for the blunder in an article dated April 6, 2011. It was simply preposterous.

On September 5, 2013, a documentary film titled "Cheonan Project" was released. It was mostly about trying to debunk the civilian-military joint investigation team's conclusion that the ship Cheonan sunk as the result of a North Korean torpedo attack. Five families of the Cheonan victims filed a motion to ban the release of the Cheonan Project, but Uijeongbu District Court dismissed the case. The court explained that the case was dismissed because "the production and release of a movie is protected under the constitutional freedom of speech." It was the cause of many controversies and conflicts, but the film was a big failure in theaters with only 21,317 ticket sales.

Years later in 2018, the Cheonan Sinking became a subject of controversy again in South Korea when the Ministry of Unification announced on February 22, 2018 that "the North Korean government has sent notice that a group of high-level North Korean delegates are visiting South Korea to attend the closing ceremony of the Pyeongchang Winter Olympics, and Kim Young-chul, the vice chairman of the North Korean Workers' Party, is part of the delegation group." The problem was that Kim Young-chul was the mastermind behind the Cheonan Sinking. The Ministry of Defense knew that the submarine that launched the torpedo attack at Cheonan belonged to the North Korea's Reconnaissance Bureau of the General Staff Department, and Kim Young-chul was the head of the Bureau at the time of the attack. Song Young-moo, the Minister of Defense during the President Moon Jae-in administration, also confirmed when he was testifying in front of the National Defense Committee of the National Assembly on February 28, 2018 that "North Korea is responsible for the Cheonan Sinking that happened in 2010, and the North Korean submarine that attacked and sank Cheonan belonged to the North's Reconnaissance Bureau of the General Staff Department." That means it was a fact even the Moon Jae-in administration could not refute.

Nevertheless, MBC aired a report on its prime-time news program 8 O'clock News Desk on February 23, 2018, as if they couldn't care less about the victims and surviving families of the Cheonan Sinking incident. The report was titled, "Kim Young-chul is suspected but not confirmed as the mastermind behind the Cheonan Sinking… Dialogue is Possible" (by Um Ji-in)

I could not believe what I was watching. Do they really have a good reason to defend the North's Kim Young-chul to the point of being so absurd? The report went on:

A multi-national investigation team which included the United States and Great Britain concluded in 2010 that Cheonan sank after being attacked by a North Korean torpedo.

The Ministry of Defense added that it was likely that the North's Reconnaissance Bureau of the General Staff Department was behind the Cheonan Sinking Incident.

Hwang Won-dong, the then-chief of intelligence at the Defense Ministry, May 2010
"Considering similar precedent cases, they believe there is a good possibility that the North's Reconnaissance Bureau of the General Staff Department pulled off this attack as well."

Based on these statements, Kim Young-chul is often pointed out as the mastermind behind the attack because he was the head of the Bureau at the time. But in official reports, there is nothing that verifies Kim Young-chul's involvement in the incident, and his name is not even mentioned in the report. It is because there is no solid proof.

The point of the report was that Kim Young-chul could not be confirmed as the mastermind behind the Cheonan Sinking because of the lack of solid proof that confirmed the attack was pulled off by the Bureau. The North is a state where nobody can walk in and investigate. Therefore, the claim of not being able to confirm the culprit for the lack of solid proof should not be applied to cases involving North Korea at least. Did the international joint investigation team fail to find solid proof even though the North fully cooperated in their investigation? Even though it is their duty for the press to raise questions continuously, reporting that defends the North's Kim Young-chul should never be accepted, particularly when it comes to the public broadcasting company of the South.

Then the question is: What motivated MBC to air such a report? I wonder if it was because of the position of Moon Jae-in's government on the issue and MBC was simply trying to support Moon's administration. Regarding Kim Young-chul's visit to the South, Moon Jae-in's government stated, "We ask for your understanding from a broad point of view." It came from the Ministry of Unification spokesperson Baek Tae-hyun on the morning of February 23, 2018. He went on to say,

"It is true that the North is clearly behind the sinking of Cheonan and that Kim Young-chul was the head of the North's Reconnaissance Bureau of the General Staff Department at the time of the attack, but it is also true that there is a limit in pointing to a specific person involved in the incident."

In short, the spokesperson was asking us to understand it from a broad point of view for the sake of improving South-North relationship even though the controversy over Kim Young-chul was growing. But he went a step further and claimed, "we cannot confirm whether Kim Young-chul was truly the mastermind behind the Cheonan Sinking."

This statement from the Ministry of Unification came out on the morning of February 23, and the MBC report was aired in the evening of the same day. Given the timeframe, I cannot shake off the feeling that MBC was dancing with the Moon Jae-in administration when it aired the report. As a journalist, it hurt because I felt I was witnessing a reality where a public broadcasting company of South Korea was trying to flatter

South Korean singers performed in Pyongyang. The South's popular girl band Red Velvet's member Irene became the talk of the town after taking a photo standing next to Kim Jong-un.

the left-wing government.

MBC might have tried to show its loyalty to the Moon Jae-in administration, but it had egg on its face when the Minister of Defense Song Young-moo testified at the National Defense Committee of the National Assembly on February 28, "I am aware that the North Korean submarine that was sent at the time of the Cheonan Sinking belonged to the North's Reconnaissance Bureau of the General Staff Department." When asked what he thought about Kim Young-chul's visit to the South, he stated, "From the perspective of the military personnel, I find it offensive." I was relieved to find that such an outspoken minister with principle was part of the Moon Jae-in administration. Still, I could not stop thinking that MBC's report was truly outrageous.

With the Moon Jae-in government and the Korean press demonstrating that kind of attitude, I wonder how much the North must be disdaining the South. I don't think I have to see to know the answer. On March

31, 2018, a group of Korean entertainers including the singers Cho Yong-phil, Lee Sun-hee, Yoon Do-hyun, and Red Velvet visited Pyongyang for an event called "Concert of South Korean Performers in Pyongyang to Wish for Peaceful Cooperation Between the South and the North," which lasted until April 4. During this concert period, Kim Young-chul committed an audacious act. On April 2, the day when the singers were having a concert in Pyongyang, Kim Young-chul had a meeting with a group of journalists from the South and introduced himself by saying, "I am Kim Young-chul, the one accused of having masterminded the sinking of Cheonan in the South." He was saying that to taunt those in the South who were accusing him. Many Koreans in the South were outraged when they learned about this episode through the media.

When the controversy continued to grow, the Ministry of Unification made a statement two days later on April 4, in response to Kim Young-chul, who was the vice-chairman of the Central Committee of the Workers' Party of Korea for South Korean affairs and head of the United Front Work Department at the time, and the way he introduced himself "I am Kim Young-chul, the one being accused of having masterminded the sinking of Cheonan in the South." In the statement, the Ministry of Unification spokesperson said, "We have trust in the report the Ministry of Defense has made." The Ministry of Defense continued to hold the position that they could not identify the mastermind of the Cheonan Sinking. On February 28, the defense minister Song Young-moo announced that "the North Korean submarine that attacked and sank Cheonan belonged to the North's Reconnaissance Bureau of the General Staff Department." Given that, I cannot understand what nonsense the Ministry of Unification and the Ministry of Defense were talking when they said they could not identify Kim Young-chul, the then head of the Reconnaissance

Kim Young-chul, the then-head of the North's Reconnaissance Bureau, was accused of having masterminded the Cheonan Sinking.

Bureau, as the mastermind of the Cheonan Sinking. Kim Young-chul could boldly make a taunting remark because the Moon Jae-in government is being so servile to the North, making those in the North disdain those in the South.

On July 5, the Korean national basketball team visited Pyongyang, North Korea, for an event called the "Unification Basketball Tournament". Kim Young-chul visited the Pyongyang Koryo Hotel where the Minster of Unification Cho Myung-gyun was staying with the national basketball team. On his way to the hotel, he was asked by reporters from the South, "Why did you introduce yourself to the reporters in April as the one accused of being the mastermind behind the Cheonan Sinking?" But he simply passed by them without giving an answer. To Kim Young-chul who looks down on the South Korean government, the reporters from the South might also have seemed like nothing but nuisances he could simply ignore.

6-9.
THE PRESS ACCUSES FISHERMEN OF RESPONSIBILITY FOR THE SECOND BATTLE OF YEONPYEONG

On June 29, 2002, when the entire country was swept up in the fever over the Korea-Japan World Cup match, two North Korean patrol boats sent a barrage of fire at the ROK Navy patrol boat PKM-357, killing six including Lt. Cmdr. Yoon Young-ha and Han Sang-guk. But this military clash did not upset the left-wing Kim Dae-jung administration, which was advocating an amicable South-North relationship. Instead of responding to the incident, President Kim Dae-jung left for Yokohama, Japan, to watch the final match of the World Cup soccer between Brazil and Germany.

Then on June 30, MBC started to carry out a slew of reporting activities that were hard to comprehend. First, there was their arrangement of news stories that didn't make much sense. The news stories from the first to the eighth were all about the World Cup final. That meant MBC had as many as eight news stories about the World Cup final match — not even between Korea and Japan, but between Brazil and Germany. The news about the battle of Yeonpyeong (which at the time was called the

President Kim Dae-jung and his wife left for Yokohama, Japan, to watch the World Cup final match the day after the Battle of Yeonpyeong.

West Sea Battle) came as the 9th news story. On the same day, KBS made 22 stories about the battle their top news reports, and the news about the World Cup final was aired as the 23rd, which was the more common-sense reporting order. SBS started off the day's news program with a three-minute highlight of the World Cup final match, before starting 13 stories about the battle of Yeonpyeong, followed by news coverage of the World Cup match as the 14th story.

The problem was the way MBC arranged the news reports. On this particular day, MBC reporters demonstrated a rather bizarre suggestion that they were telling stories from the perspectives of the North.

"The North Accusing the South of Having Violated Territorial Waters in Connection with the West Sea Battle" (by Lee Yong-ma)

The report was about how the North was categorically refuting the claims made by the South. It would have been understandable if the point of the report was about the claims made by the North. KBS and SBS did in fact report exclusively about the claims made by the North. But the report by MBC was not about the North's claims only.

- Reporter: The attitude of North Korea corroborates the analysis that concluded this incident was not intentional provocation by the North. Besides, it is difficult to agree that the North intentionally created this incident at a time when the Arirang Festival is going on and the US-North talks are to take place shortly.

- Seo Dong-man (Professor of Sangji University): It is hard to describe it as an intentional act where the top leadership including the North's Chairman of the National Defense Commission Kim Jong-il are involved.

Reporter Lee Yong-ma went one step further to claim that it was very likely that the North was telling the truth. I cannot understand on what grounds he made that claim. He even brought in Seo Dong-man, the professor from Sangji University, in an apparent attempt to defend the North. For your reference, Professor Seo is a leftist who was sent to prison in the 1970s on charges of having participated in the student movement, and in April 2003, shortly after the inception of the Roh Moo-hyun administration, he became the director of the Office of Planning & Coordination of National Intelligence Service. After he became the director, he was continuously accused of being a pro-North leftist.

On July 1, MBC aired reports that were hard to comprehend beginning with its top news story.

"Yeonpyeong Island Crab Fishermen Blame Themselves for the West Sea Battle" (by Yoo Sang-ha)

Even though it was a battle provoked by the North Korean soldiers, killing many of our soldiers, MBC reported in its headline news that "the engagement had happened because of some crab fishermen." The content of the report was as follows:

- Reporter: According to the testimony of fishermen, there were 56 boats that had permission to fish on the day of the battle, and six Navy vessels were monitoring them.
  But ten among those fishing boats were so focused on their work that they ended up violating maritime boundaries.
- Shin Nam-seok (Yeonpyeong-do resident): When our boats were sailing beyond the designated fishing zone and about to cross a disputed maritime boundary, our Navy's patrol boats tried to stop them to protect us fishermen.
- Reporter: Our Navy quickly guided the fishing boats back to the south, but a couple of boats ignored the Navy's command and sailed away, forcing our patrol boats to speed up to chase them.
- Shin Nam-seok (Yeonpyeong-do resident): Our patrol boats kept urging those fishermen to turn and sail back to south when the North Korean patrol boats started firing.
- Reporter: The witnesses unanimously testified that the engagement happened when the North's patrol boats suddenly appeared during the chase.

On this day, MBC aired four news reports in a row about how the crab fishing boats caused such a devastating event.

#1: Yeonpyeong-do crab fishermen testify that they caused the West Sea Battle (by Yoo Sang-ha)

#2: Yeonpyeong-do crab fishermen fish beyond the maritime boundary

(by Hwang Seok-ho)

#3: Fatal consequences for Navy patrol boats controlling crab fishing boats (by Chun Bong-gi)

#4: Statement by the Ministry of Defense Does Not Match Fishermen's Testimony (by Park Seung-jin)

MBC continued to report that 'the cause of the Second Battle of Yeonpyeong was the illegal fishing of crab fishermen.' Those reports were completely different from the ones by KBS and SBS. While this was going on, KBS reported on July 5, 2002 about the on-site investigation of the Second Battle of Yeonpyeong by the Joint Chiefs of Staff.

"Problem with the Navy's Initial Response" (by Kwon Jae-min)

- Reporter: There are claims that our fishermen have violated the maritime boundary, thereby causing the engagement on the ocean, but the authorities reportedly concluded that their fishing activities had nothing to do with the engagement.

The "claims" mentioned in this KBS report are believed to refer to the MBC news reports. Monthly Chosun also reported in its August 2002 edition, "The MBC News Desk is losing viewer ratings and turning its viewers away by misleading them in saying that the trigger of the battle in the West Sea was the crab boats that violated the maritime boundary, not provocation by the North." In response to the magazine's article, MBC filed a defamation lawsuit against Monthly Chosun, and asked for indemnification for damage. But the Seoul Central District Court made a decision in favor of Monthly Chosun. In its decision, the court ruled that "when Monthly Chosun printed the article, it was within the boundary of fair 'criticism' between news media outlets, and therefore did not damage the reputation of the plaintiff." The court also ruled, "Considering the influence a public broadcasting company has on public opinion, a liberal and broad criticism about the objectivity and fairness of broadcast reports has to be allowed."

6-10.

JTBC PLAYS A LEADING ROLE IN INCITING ISSUES REGARDING THE US THAAD DEPLOYMENT

At a breakfast forum hosted by the Korea Institute of Defense Analysis (KIDA) that took place on June 3, 2014, the U.S. Forces Korea commander, Lt. Gen. Curtis Scaparrotti stated that he personally recommended that the Korean government agree to the THAAD deployment. Soon after, Korea was swept up in heated arguments over the deployment.

THAAD is a defense tool that South Korea must have to counter the North's ballistic missiles. Terminal High Altitude Area Defense (THAAD) is an anti-ballistic missile defense system designed to intercept and shoot down ballistic missiles at up to a 3,000km range with altitudes of 40-150km. Prior to THAAD, Patriot was the main anti-ballistic missile defense system available in the South. Patriot is capable of shooting down ballistic missiles at altitudes of 15-30km. We need to note that THAAD can intercept missiles at up to 150km, and Patriot, up to 30km. If we have both THAAD and Patriot, South Korea will have a dual defense system: If a ballistic missile is not intercepted in the first phase, Patriot can intercept and shoot it down at a lower altitude in the second phase.

The Patriot missile defense system that the ROC Air Force has is the PAC-2 version, which is designed to spew out metal fragments aimed at tearing up an incoming missile, instead of directly intercepting and shooting it down. The problem was that its method and success rate have always remained questionable. Therefore, there have been ongoing efforts to upgrade and improve it to a new PAC-3 version that can directly hit and shoot down the missiles of enemies. This proves how important the THAAD deployment is for Korea's national defense.

At a time when a dynamic discussion existed over THAAD deployment for the protection of the South Korean people from the North's ballistic missiles, China abruptly stepped in and opposed the deployment. On February 4, 2015, the Chinese Minister of Defense Chang Wanquan made threatening remarks during the Korea-China defense ministers talks and said, "The Korea-China relationship will be damaged if THAAD is deployed in the Korean Peninsula." His point was that the THAAD deployment was not intended to contain the North: it was intended to contain China.

The objection of China cooled the debate over the THAAD deployment, but it started picking up again in 2016. On January 13, 2016, President Park Geun-hye stated in her New Year's public speech that she was "going to consider the THAAD deployment in the interests of national security." China started voicing their objections on February 15 using such dramatic expressions as "resolute objection." Hong Lei, the spokesperson for the Chinese Ministry of Foreign Affairs, criticized both the United States and South Korea, saying "We are deeply concerned about the possible THAAD deployment in the Korean Peninsula…We resolutely object to the attempt to take advantage of the Korean Peninsula issues to damage the national security and interests of China." Under this

6. EXAMPLES OF THE KOREAN PRESS SEIZED BY THE KOREA CONFEDERATION OF TRADE UNIONS

circumstance, Korean leftist lawmakers from the Democratic Party of Korea, People's Party, and Justice Party went along with the Chinese position and started criticizing the US and South Korean governments.

The whole situation seemed to make the chronically pathological anti-Americanism to flourish all over again. The Korean press has always played a big contributing role in fueling the anti-American sentiment in Korea. One example was a shocking JTBC exclusive report titled "USFK carries out Zika virus experiment in the middle of Seoul city" that was aired on May 11, 2016. The title itself was enough to terrorize and anger Koreans. As I mentioned previously, a group called Green Korea terrorized and enraged Koreans by claiming that the USFK had secretly released formaldehyde into the Han River on July 14, 2000. This controversy continued until the movie director Bong Joon-ho released a movie titled "Host" in July 2006.

JTBC has been a full-pledged left-wing broadcasting company since Sohn Suk-hee was appointed the JTBC president. I will talk about later the ironic situation in which JTBC, a broadcasting company owned by a large corporation, has become a left-wing broadcasting company. Originally, Sohn Suk-hee had joined MBC as an announcer. He is a radical leftist as proved by his background: He was serving as an executive at the Korea Confederation of Trade Unions-affiliated National Union of Media Workers when he participated in a strike in October 1992 and was arrested.

When Sohn Suk-hee's JTBC aired the report about the USFK carrying out a Zika virus experiment in the middle of Seoul city, the USFK immediately denied it. The next day on May 12, the USFK announced that the report was not true at all, and that it was a mistake caused by JTBC that mistranslated an English paragraph found on a website. The paragraph at issue was found on the website of Edgewood Chemical Biological Center (ECBC), and it went as follows:

"The participants in the project are already looking to add a Zika virus detection capability in Yongsan." said Redmond.

It was a simple sentence that could easily be translated: Dr. Redmond is saying that the project participants were expecting to add a Zika virus detection capability at the US base in Yongsan. But to everybody's shock, the JTBC reporters and editorial desk mistranslated a very simple English sentence and reported it as if it was their scoop. According to their report, Dr. Redmond gave instructions to add a Zika virus-related program in Yongsan. Instead of reporting that there were people expecting to add a Zika virus detecting capability in Yongsan, JTBC accused the USFK of carrying out a Zika virus experiment in the middle of Seoul city.

But the misinformation from JTBC immediately resulted in nationwide anti-American rage, even though there were people who pointed out that the report was not true. While this was going on, the South Korean and the US governments made an official announcement on July 8, 2016 that the decision was made to deploy THAAD to Korea. A few days later on the 13th, the government made another announcement that the Seongsan artillery unit in Seongsan-ri, Seongju-gun, North Gyeongsang Province had been selected as the THAAD site. On that very day, Moon Jae-in, the leading presidential candidate and the former leader of the Democratic Party of Korea, stated on his Facebook page that "Collaboration and cooperating diplomacy with surrounding countries are necessary to solve issues with the North." And he went on to say, "The THAAD deployment is an issue that needs reconsideration," indicating that he objected to the THAAD deployment. The "surrounding countries" Moon Jae-in mentioned in his statement refers to China, because Japan already expressed their approval of the THAAD deployment.

On this very day when Moon Jae-in revealed he was against the THAAD deployment, JTBC aired yet another absurd report. It was titled, "The problem with the THAAD radar that is pointing at civilian houses... The situation of the Japanese base" reported by Yoo Seon-ui and aired during the JTBC prime-time news program Newsroom. In this report, JTBC committed another embarrassing mistake of mistranslating part of an article published on January 10, 2016 in the Stars and Stripes, which is an American military newspaper.

The sentence at issue read as follows:

"Site Armadillo feels remote because it is ... and the roar of a massive generator that could light a small town envelops all."

It is another simple sentence about Site Armadillo, and how it feels remote and that all is enveloped by the roar of a generator that is massive enough to light a small town.

But JTBC reported a mistranslated version, which indicated, "The roar of the generator is enough to envelop the entire small village" While the Stars and Stripes article was stressing how the THAAD was based in a remote village in the jungle, JTBC changed it to mean how tremendous the noise from THAAD was. Their mistranslation didn't end there.

"The site is bounded by densely wooded Conservation Area No. 50 on one side. The only thing that we know lives in there are two pigs, Pork Chop and Bacon Bit."

Lawmakers Sohn Hye-won (l.) and Pyo Chang-won (r.) are dancing to the song about protesting against the deployment of THAAD.

It is yet another simple and easy paragraph to understand. With the high level of English education available in Korea, almost all Koreans can tell what this simple English paragraph is about. Yet, the JTBC reporters and news desk didn't report it as it was, either because their English was substandard, or they intended to mislead the viewers.

JTBC said in its report that "the only thing that can live in this area are two pigs." Even though the original report was about an area so remote that only thing that they knew lived there were two pigs, JTBC made it sound provocative by translating it as "an area where only two pigs could live" due to the THAAD site.

Eventually, JTBC admitted "There was some mistranslation in our report" and made an official apology on July 17, 2016, four days after its first report. On August 25, 2016, the Korea Communications Standards Commission issued a warning to JTBC for the report, which was a heavy punishment equivalent to a sanction by the court.

But by then, anti-American sentiment was already widely spread throughout the left-wing camp. On August 3, 2016, six lawmakers from the Democratic Party of Korea including Pyo Chang-won, Sohn Hye-won, and Park Joo-min visited Seongju to participate in the "candlelight rally" to protest the THAAD deployment. During the rally, Pyo Chang-won and Sohn Hye-won committed the atrocity of terrifying people by singing a song together whose lyrics went, "THAAD releases dangerous electromagnetic waves." Their behavior clearly showed how substandard the members of the Korean National Assembly really were. The original title of the song that they sang was "Night After Night" by Insooni. But they changed the lyrics to meet their needs. The changed lyrics went as follows:

"Night after night, I hate the electromagnetic waves of THAAD …. I hate it because the strong electromagnetic waves seem to rip my body apart."

These pathetic leftist lawmakers didn't stop there. They also sang "What About My Age" by Oh Seung-geun, and this time, they changed the lyrics as follows:

"One day I just happened to notice how my body had been fried by electromagnetic waves"

This shows what kind of people the members of the Korean National Assembly really are. They find nothing wrong with instigating people with ridiculous metaphors likening soldiers serving in the THAAD base to bodies being fried inside a microwave. A year later, on August 12, 2017, test results confirmed that both the electromagnetic waves and noise coming from the THAAD base were harmless to the human body, but they faced even more criticism because they had never bothered to apologize for what they had done.

Sohn Hye-won and other lawmakers from the Democratic Party of Korea who had danced and sang to instigate terror in the people at THAAD on August 3, 2016 went to China eight days later on the 15th. The six lawmakers including Sohn Hye-won and Kim Young-ho stated that they went to Beijing to hear the opinion of Chinese officials about the THAAD that was scheduled to be deployed in Korea. This incident was more than just a humiliating act of diplomacy: It could be even considered an act of threatening the national security of Korea. Why were they compelled to seek the opinions of Chinese officials over the THAAD deployment, which was all about protecting Korea from the North's ballistic missiles? Their toadying diplomacy with China didn't stop there. On January 4, 2017, seven lawmakers from the Democratic Party of Korea including Song Young-gil and Park Jeong had a meeting with China's Vice Foreign Minister Wang Yi. Around this time, China was already taunting Korean companies, including Lotte, as their "retaliation over the THAAD deployment," yet those lawmakers were only there to listen to the reasons China was objecting the THAAD deployment in Korea, and they did not say a word condemning China for taunting Korean companies.

Perhaps JTBC is the most dangerous left-wing media outlet in Korea. It is the most dangerous because, unlike Hankyoreh, Kyunghyang, and Hankook newspapers, JTBC has a broadcasting media and is owned by a large corporation. On top of that, JTBC is extremely audacious and shameless. The JTBC exclusive report "Choi Soon-sil's PC is Found…She Received Every Speech by the President" (by Kim Phil-joon) dated October 24, 2016 ended up changing the fate of Korea. In this report, JTBC claimed it had acquired "Choi Soon-sil's computer files." And the report also used the term "PC" to indicate a computer. JTBC even showed the image that anyone would have recognized as a list of files you can see on a computer monitor.

Then people started raising questions about how JTBC gained access to Choi Soon-sil's computer files. According to *The Curses of Sohn Suk-hee* (2017) written by Byun Hee-jae, JTBC used the term "Choi Soon-sil's computer files" in its exclusive report dated October 24, 2016, and then changed it to "Choi Soon-sil's Tablet PC" beginning two days later on October 26. I don't know what it's like in other countries, but in Korea, people rarely refer to a tablet PC as a computer. It is the same with smartphones: a smartphone may share some features with a computer, but people don't refer to a smartphone as a computer. Given that, it is hard to understand how JTBC confused tablet PC with computer, particularly in such a significant exclusive report. Suspicions over JTBC kept growing when people realized that JTBC's statements on how they were able to acquire Choi Soon-sil's tablet PC did not add up. Since the issue requires very complicated explanations, I ask readers to read Byun Hee-jae's *The Curses of Sohn Suk-hee* if you are interested about it.

On December 9, 2016, the Korean National Assembly passed a bill to impeach President Park Geun-hye. It was possible because a significant number of lawmakers from the ruling Liberty Party of Korea voted in favor of the bill. On the very same day, Sohn Suk-hee, the president of the JTBC news reporting division and the anchor of its prime-time news program Newsroom, made an absurd comment, which was even shown on the screen in big letters: "Perhaps such a thing as a tablet PC might not even have been necessary."

JTBC started downplaying the significance of the tablet PC when its admissibility as evidence was questioned.

JTBC's report, dated October 24, 2016, ultimately resulted in the impeachment of President Park Geun-hye. Given that, is that what he can say as the president of the JTBC news reporting division that wrote up that report? Even though the President was impeached because of the tablet PC?

Then one might wonder: Who is Sohn Suk-hee's boss? His boss is Hong Jeongdo, who is in his 40s and a third generation of a chaebol family. Hong Jeongdo is the president of both Joongang Daily and JTBC. Hong Jeongdo's grandfather is Hong Jin-ki, who founded Joongang Daily and a broadcasting company named TBC, and was also a legislative officer working at the Legislative Division of the US army military government in Korea. Hong Jin-ki's daughter, Hong Ra-hee is the wife of Samsung Chairman Lee Kun-hee, and their son is current Samsung Vice President. Hong Ra-hee's younger brother is Hong Seok-hyun, who was appointed the Korean Ambassador to the United States during the left-wing Roh Moo-hyun administration in February 2005. Being a second generation of a chaebol family and the Korean Ambassador to the United States during the left-wing administration, he was considered to be the

6. EXAMPLES OF THE KOREAN PRESS SEIZED BY THE KOREA CONFEDERATION OF TRADE UNIONS

next presidential candidate who would succeed Roh Moo-hyun. But after MBC aired an investigative report titled "Samsung X File Incident", Hong Seok-hyun was implicated in the case and had to resign from his post as the Korean Ambassador to the United States in just seven months. The Samsung X File incident was about Hong Seok-hyun, the then-president of Joongang Daily, conspiring with Samsung Group Vice-Chairman Lee Hak-soo in Shilla Hotel in 1997 to raise funds to help a specific presidential candidate and also bribing prosecutors. The winner of the 1997 presidential election was Kim Dae-jung.

After having his dream of becoming president crushed and also having to resign the post of Korean Ambassador to the United States

Hong Jeongdo is claiming that uncorroborated facts are also valuable information.

in just seven months because of the Samsung X File Incident, perhaps Hong Seok-hyun is expecting his son Hong Jeongdo to pick up where he left off. Hong Jeongdo, a man in his 40s and the third generation of a chaebol family, made a speech at the 50th Anniversary Joongang Media Conference that took place in Dongdaemun Design Plaza, Seoul, on September 21, 2015. Addressing the future vision of the company, Hong Jeongdo said, with the title of his speech displayed on the big screen, "Uncorroborated facts are also valuable information."

"If you are a journalist with the right ethics of journalism, how can you write facts that haven't been checked?"

"This is something that is really difficult to accept for journalists, but the truth is, it is what needs to be changed."

"And I am confident that we can survive in the changing media environment of the future only when we manage the trend of news in this way."

As a journalist, I wish I could just curse at him. I wonder if there is any worse president of a media outlet than him — and more audacious and shameless than him. With the president of JTBC so audacious to talk about the ethics of journalism and then claim "we can survive in the changing media environment of future only when we manage the trend of news in this way even if the facts are unchecked," his subordinate Sohn Suk-hee must have felt it was okay for him to say something as outrageous and nonsensical as, "Perhaps such a thing as a tablet PC might not have even been necessary."

Perhaps the most disgusting group of people in Korea must be the so-called "Gangnam Leftists." Gangnam refers to the district south of the Han River, which is comparatively more affluent than Gangbuk, the north of the river. "Gangnam Leftist" is a term Koreans use to criticize

6. EXAMPLES OF THE KOREAN PRESS SEIZED BY THE KOREA CONFEDERATION OF TRADE UNIONS

Trump points a JTBC reporter and jokes he is a pro-government journalist.

those who were born with a silver spoon and are acting like they are liberal leftists. Wouldn't Hong Jeongdo qualify as the typical Gangnam leftist? Hong Jeongdo was hired by Joongang Daily in May 2005 as an employee belonging to the strategic planning team of the newspaper, but he was promoted to the director of the team in less than four years in January 2009, and then continued to move up the corporate ladder each year until he became a managing director. It was ten years after he first joined the company that he became the president of both JTBC and Joongang Daily. Would it have been possible had he not been a third generation of a chaebol family?

On May 22, 2018, US President Donald Trump had a meeting with President Moon Jae-in in the White House. President Trump gestured to appreciate the reporters and asked them to leave the office since the open question and answer time was up. The White House staffers were also telling reporters to leave the office loudly. However, President Moon kept taking questions from a Korean reporter who was sitting to his right, perhaps because he didn't understand English. Watching this, President Trump joked, pointing his finger at the reporter,

"He is a pro-government reporter. These two are close."

It was a remark made by President Trump about the situation where President Moon Jae-in and the reporter were asking and answering as if they were following a script. The reporter in this incident was Ko Seok-seung from JTBC. Of course, I don't believe President Trump knew that the reporter was from JTBC when he made that joke. It was a funny coincidence where the "pro-government reporter" that President Trump joked about turned out to be actually a reporter from JTBC. Numerous Internet users had a lot of fun posting and sharing photos and videos of the incident on social media.

| 6-11.

THE KOREAN PRESS SIDING WITH THE NORTH BLAMING THE UNITED STATES

The South and the North were scheduled to have a high-level meeting at 10:00am, May 16, 2018. However, just after midnight at around 0:30am on the very same day, the North notified that the South-North high-level meeting was postponed indefinitely. The North explained that the meeting was postponed because of Max Thunder, which was a joint U.S.–South Korean military exercise. Korea and the US Air Force had been doing Max Thunder since 2009. The two-week long exercise — which started on May 11, 2018 and was to end on May 25 — involved over 100 aircrafts from both countries including eight F-22 Raptors, F-15, and F-16. The exercise had already started on May 11 when the North announced that the high-level meeting between the South and North was postponed indefinitely in the early morning of the 16th, using Max Thunder as the excuse.

Then in its prime-time main news program "9 O'clock News," KBS aired a report about its analysis on the reason the North changed its position out of the blue. The title and the content of the report are as follows:

"The North Reacts Head-on to the Hard-lined Comment of a US Official – Are South-North Relations Going to Take a Break?" (by Yoon Jin)

"According to an analysis, the North is expressing its dissatisfaction because the United States is bringing up the denuclearization issue, which is an essential agenda item, as well as biochemical weapons, mid-to-long range missiles, Japanese kidnappings, and even human rights issues that the North is sensitive about."

"It seems that the North felt compelled to make a strong warning after John Bolton, a White House national security adviser, said he was planning to bring North Korea's nuclear weapons to Oak Ridge, Tennessee, where Libyan nuclear equipment was stored, and destroy them there."

"The United States is not saying a single word about the North's demands about issues including the abolishment of hostile policies and guarantee of system security."

The point of the report was that the United States caused the North to demonstrate such a dissatisfied reaction. On this day, MBC aired a report about the claims made by the North's vice foreign minister Kim Kye-gwan who criticized the United States, and SBS did similar reporting. However, KBS aired a report in the form of an analysis that it did on its own, instead of reporting Kim Kye-gwan's claims. The difference is big from the perspective of the viewers. KBS — the biggest public broadcasting company in Korea — reported an analysis that indicated the North had postponed the meeting indefinitely largely because of the radical statement made by a US official. KBS Public Broadcasters Union

— which is a counter union for the KCTU-affiliated NUM headquarters — made a statement pointing out the problems with the report. In the statement titled "How Is the US Responsible for the North's Cancellation" the union strongly criticized KBS by claiming, "There is nothing in this report about the North's whim, deception, or genuine commitment to denuclearization. Instead, it is all about blaming the US for the North's repulsion and cancellation of the meeting."

6-12.

MBC IS UNCOMFORTABLE WITH THE EXPRESSION OF "THE NORTH IS OUR ENEMY"

On June 25, 2018, MBC aired a sheer nonsense report. June 25 is the day when the Korean War broke out. On June 25, 1950, the North Korean forces of 198,380 soldiers crossed the 38th parallel all at once and invaded the South. During the three-years-one-month war that ended when the Armistice Agreement was signed on July 27, 1953, more than one million Korean civilians lost their lives. The South Korean forces sustained 138,000 fatalities and 450,000 injuries, but if those who were never located were included, the total casualties reached about 609,000. The United Nations Forces that came to our rescue from distant countries sustained 58,000 fatalities and 150,000 injuries, but if the number of the missing and the captives was included, the total casualties were over 480,000.

On this day, MBC aired a report that raised issues over the "June 25 Song" which the people sang together in the ceremony to commemorate the 68th anniversary of the Korean War. The title and the content of the report is as follows:

6. EXAMPLES OF THE KOREAN PRESS SEIZED BY THE KOREA CONFEDERATION OF TRADE UNIONS

The Korean War left millions of deaths and injuries.

"The Enemy and the Barbarians …. Singing the June 25 Song" (by Yoo Choong-hwan)

"When the June 25 song started, all attendees including Prime Minister Lee Nak-yeon joined and sang along."

"However, the song has a line that says the North is our enemy…. 'stop the enemy with fist and red blood.'"

"The words become more radical."

"Now we will bring revenge to the enemies of that day."

"We will fight and defeat each and every enemy."

"The song is about paying respect to our veterans and our commitment to never forgetting the pain of the war, but there are people who claim that the expressions are uncomfortable to hear."

"There are people who point out that we need to change the lyrics to make the song more appropriate for this time of peace and reconciliation."

The report was outrageous beyond word, but the pathetic MBC reporter aired it in its main prime-time news program. Is the expression "uncomfortable reaction" the creation of the reporter himself? Did he conduct a poll surveying all of South Korea? Is the war that started by the North's invasion and left one million civilian fatalities a war that we have to forget now? Was he in his right mind when he reported that the song lyrics had to be revised to make it more appropriate for this time of peace and reconciliation? How can he face the United Nations Command (UNC) soldiers, including the Americans, who came from distant lands to protect our country? The MBC labor union that is a counter organization against the KCTU-affiliated NUM made a statement on June 26 and pointed out the following issues in regards to the report.

"Let us march! May impure blood water our fields!" — Those are lines from 'La Marseillaise,' which is the national anthem of France. Are the French people singing this song because they are in the time of war? We are concerned because we never know what kind of song lyrics the MBC news desk is going to advocate on June 25 next year.

I am deeply concerned about President Moon Jae-in's ostentatious flattery to the North to create harmonious South-North relations. And I am flabbergasted at how MBC, the second largest national television network only following after KBS in Korea, is being so servile to the North as well.

6-13.

THE KOREAN PRESS ACCUSES THE US VICE PRESIDENT MIKE PENCE FOR BEING RUDE

On February 9, 2018, US Vice President Mike Pence attended the Pyeongchang Winter Olympic Reception and left the venue five minutes later. Many Korean news outlets criticized his hasty exit and claimed the Vice President Pence did "a diplomatic discourtesy".

- Yonhap News Agency: Vice President Pence Avoids the North's Kim Young-nam Disregarding Diplomatic Courtesy — Drawing the Line at the US-North Dialogue (by Kim Seong-wook, Park Kyung-joon)
- Hankyoreh: Rudeness of Pence... Shakes Hands Except with Kim Young-nam, Exits Immediately After Reception (by Seong Yeon-cheol)
- Kookmin Ilbo: Pence Ends Up Not Joining the Reception... Criticized for His Diplomatic Discourtesy (by Kang Joon-gu, Kwon Ji-hye)
- Financial News: Pence and Abe Do Diplomatic Discourtesy at President Moon's Reception to Avoid the North's Kim Young-nam (by Cho Eun-hyo)

First off, we need to understand the reason US Vice President Mike Pence left the reception venue after five minutes. Pence had allegedly requested the presidential Blue House of Korea before his arrival to "ensure my schedule would not cross paths with the North's Kim Young-nam." Kim Young-nam is the President of the Presidium of the Supreme People's Assembly of North Korea, and he ranks number two in power following only after Kim Jong-un in the North. Since the United States and the North were in conflicting relations at the time, Pence had asked Moon Jae-in's government not to make him shake hands or cross paths with the man second in power in the North.

Despite his request, the Moon Jae-in administration arranged for US Vice President Pence to sit at the same head table with the North's Kim Young-nam. It showed how the Moon's administration blatantly ignored Pence's request. I believe Pence's act was justified considering how rude the Moon's administration was to him. The Korean press criticized Pence for being rude and having done a diplomatic discourtesy, but it was the Moon Jae-in administration that was being rude to him. In the end, Vice President Pence took photos with President Moon Jae-in and the Japanese Prime Minister Shinzo Abe, shook hands with leaders from other countries, and left the venue five minutes later. As you can imagine, he did not shake hands with the North's Kim Young-nam.

The next day on February 10, the Liberty Korea Party made a statement and criticized the Moon Jae-in administration, claiming it was "another diplomatic disaster caused by the Moon Jae-in administration that ignored the intentions of an ally and tried to approach the US-North dialogue as a show." The Liberty Korea Party also explained, "Upon arriving in Korea, Vice President Pence toured the Cheonan Warship Exhibition Hall with North Korean defectors, and during the tour, he said their struggle for freedom was in the hearts of Americans." The Liberty Korea Party also stressed, "All Koreans and even Americans have clear awareness of the true nature of North Korea, but President Moon Jae-in and those in power with backgrounds in left-wing ideologies and student movements are simply ignoring it."

7. MOVING FORWARD TO THE ERA OF NEW MEDIA

7-1.
TRUMP DECLARES WAR ON FAKE NEWS

Americans might find it weird if a Korean is talking about what's happening in the United States. But in some ways, the situation in the United States share many similarities with that of South Korea. However, there is a big difference between the American leftists and the Korean leftists. While the American leftists tend to gear towards the enforcement of political correctness, the Korean leftists are a little more complicated. More than anything, it is inevitable for Korea to deal with special situations since the country is divided and the South and the North are in a confrontational relation, and also because NL ideologists account for a significant part of the Korean left-wing, and NL cannot be discussed without its connection with the North. Besides, the left-leaning media outlets in Korea are linked to a big labor union called the Korean Confederation of Trade Unions. All these factors result in the big difference from the left-leaning American media outlets.

Nevertheless, nobody will be able to deny that many leading media outlets in the United States are leaning towards the Left. Surely it is not fair to dichotomously define the American Democrats as the Left, and the

Republicans as the Right, but for the sake of convenience, let me follow that dichotomous definition. According to *The Political Correctness That Brought Victory to Trump* (2017) by Hong Ji-soo, the contribution made by the US journalists to the Hillary Clinton's campaign camp amounted to $383,000 as of October 2016, whereas it amounted to $14,000 for the Donald Trump's campaign camp. It makes over 27 times of difference. According to Lars Willnat and David Weaver, professors of journalism at Indiana University, the percentage of full-time U.S. journalists who claim to be Democrats was about 28 percent as of 2014, and Republicans was about 8 percent. The rest 65% of them claimed to be neutral. But the Pulitzer-winning New York Times reporter Judith Miller refuted their findings and claimed overwhelming majority of the rest 65% were leaning towards the democrats, and that it resulted in the news coverages that are seriously learning towards the Left.

Then where did the United States find solution to this problem? The solution was found not from the leading media outlets, but from the alternative media outlets. Take Andrew Breitbart, for example. Breitbart assisted Ariana Huffington in the creation of the online newspaper Huffington, where he worked as the head of the research team, and he also founded the right-wing online news website Breitbart. Breitbart was able to make success because of his interest in pop culture. Until he came around, the right-wing in the United States tended to pursue lofty ideas just like the right-wing did in Korea. However, Breitbart knew that pop culture should never be ignored when he started the Big Hollywood website to help those who did not agree to the left-wing ideology, which accounted for the majority in Hollywood. This is a lesson that Korea's right-wing alternative media outlets must learn. After winning the presidential election in 2016, Donald Trump hired Stephen K. Bannon as

White House Chief Strategist. Stephen Bannon was the former chairman of the Breitbart News. Andrew Breitbart was walking near his house in the morning in March 2012 when he collapsed. He was rushed to the hospital, where he died later. LA county coroner revealed that his autopsy showed he died of heart failure. There were many rumors surrounding his death, but it is regretful that he was a man who fought against the left-leaning major media outlets, but he didn't live to see Donald Trump's victory.

As of July 2018, the Breitbart News YouTube channel has 70,000 subscribers. Lately, however, Alex Jones Channel seems to be more popular than the Breitbart News. As of July 2018, Alex Jones YouTube channel is boasting 2.41 million subscribers.

Considering the number of subscribers of major news outlets' YouTube channels — 4.2 million for CNN, 4.1 million for ABC, 1.43 million for FOX, 810 thousand for CBS, and 770 thousand for NBC — you realize how impressive Alex Jones channel is doing online, even though it is an alternative news outlet.

7-2.

THE NEED FOR A COUNTER LABOR UNION

There is a big difference between the realities of the press in Korea and America. It is largely because there is a connecting chain called Korea Confederation of Trade Unions in Korea. Majority of Korean journalists are the members of the KCTU-affiliated National Union of Media Workers, and the public opinion in Korea is mostly directed by these member journalists.

KCTU-affiliated National Union of Media Workers (NUM) has a long history of over 30 years because it was established in 1988, the year following the 1987 June Uprising. With this long history and the support of the powerful KCTU, it is inevitable that news media outlets in Korea are under the control of the union members. In the case of MBC, NUM has a bigger influence than in any other news outlets. However, after the MBC Labor Union was established on March 6, 2013, MBC has now a pivotal group that can counter the KCTU-affiliated NUM. This is in fact a significant turn of event, because having a counter pivotal power can make a big difference. As mentioned previously, the KCTU-affiliated NUM's MBC headquarters have been struggling continuously through strikes beginning from 1988. During the right-wing Roh Tae-woo administration, MBC was on strike for 90 days in total in 1988, 1989, and 1992. During the Kim Young-sam administration — another right-wing government — MBC was on strike for 36 days in total in 1998 and 1997. Then when the left-wing Kim Dae-jung became the President, it had only one strike for 15 days, and it was to demand the overhaul of broadcasting-related laws instead of criticizing the government. Roh Moo-hyun was leaning to the Left more than Kim Dae-jung, but while he was the President, there was not a single day of strike. But when the right-wing Lee Myung-bak became the President, MBC was on strike for a whopping 232 days in total in 2008, 2009, 2010 and 2012. It means, MBC was on strike 12.7% of the five-year term of President Lee Myung-bak.

These numbers show how MBC was under the control of a powerful union, but it started to change significantly when a counter labor union was established. The MBC Labor Union was established on March 6, 2013, and the number of the union members had once reached 160. With this pivot that countered the KCTU-affiliated NUM, the MBC headquarters of NUM could hardly turn to struggle in the form of pressuring the executives with strikes like it used to in the past. On February 25, 2013, President Park Geun-hye sworn in to office, thereby realizing the inception of a government that was learning toward the Right much more than the previous Lee Myung-bak's government was. Naturally, the KCTU-affiliated NUM seemed to struggle harder than before, but their struggle did not escalate into strikes.

KCTU-affiliated NUM headquarters in MBC could not have a single strike while Park Geun-hye was in office until September 4, 2017. Moon Jae-in administration was incepted on May 10, 2017. Even though

KCTU-affiliated NUM headquarters in MBC could not have any strike during the Park Geun-hye administration, it started when the left-wing Moon Jae-in took office. The goal of the strike was to have the MBC President Kim Jang-gyum, who was appointed under the Park Geun-hye's government, dismissed. As I've mentioned previously, they were able to dismiss Kim Jang-gyum from the post as of November 13 by changing the Foundation for Broadcast Culture board members. And the NUM headquarters in MBC ended the strike on November 15, 2017, two days after Kim Jang-gyum left office.

What does it signify that they could not have a strike at all during the Park Geun-hye administration, but they did for 71 days as soon as the left-wing Moon Jae-in took office? It was because of the MBC Labor Union. The labor union with 160 members played a role in striping the NUM headquarters in MBC of the dynamics of strike, because the separate labor union made it possible to avoid broadcasting interruption even if the NUM members went on a strike. In the past, the executives of MBC had no choice but to listen to the union because a strike meant disruption in broadcasting. But MBC labor union proved that just having a counter union itself was enough to undermine the effectiveness of their random strike. However, the labor union lost its stumbling block effect after Moon Jae-in took office and the existing executives of the company were replaced with new leftist executives.

Then, what is the lesson we can learn in all of this? It is that all media outlets need a countering labor union. Without a counter union, any media outlets in Korea are destined to be controlled by the KCTU-affiliated NUM. I don't think all journalists in Korea must be the left-wing ideologists. However, in the Korean society that is ruled by seniority and age-based hierarchy, it will be difficult for younger, junior journalists to refuse to agree to a labor union where their older, senior journalists belong to as members. Koreans tend to be very conscious about the judging eyes of others. People in Japan often dine alone in restaurant but in Korea it is rare. Those who work for companies are always mindful of other workers' opinions of them. That is why a counter union is all the more necessary, because when junior and senior journalists realize they can depend on each other as members of the counter union, they can rest assured they have the right to choose.

7-3.

THE STATUS OF ALTERNATIVE JOURNALISM IN KOREA

As of today, Pen & Mike (PenN, pennmike.com) is considered the leading right-wing alternative media in Korea. PenN YouTube channel has about 220,000 subscribers as of July 2018. The right-leaning founder Chung Kyu-jae is a former reporter from the Korean Economic Daily. On February 13, 2012, he launched a one-man broadcasting outlet called Chung Kyu-jae TV while being an editorial writer of the Korean Economic Daily. He gained popularity with his brave criticism of reports made by other left-wing news outlets. However, it took a significant incident to turn the people's attention to Chung Kyu-jae TV: an exclusive interview with President Park Geun-hye aired through Chung Kyu-jae TV on January 25, 2017. The entire nation turned its attention to the interview, because it took place while the President Park Geun-hye's impeachment trial was going on at the Constitutional Court. It was an important opportunity for President Park Geun-hye to defend herself openly for the Korean people. President Park Geun-hye picked Chung Kyu-jae TV for the interview instead of broadcasting companies such as KBS, MBC, SBS or YTN, or printed media such as Chosun, Joongang or Donga. Chung

Chung Kyu-jae had an exclusive interview with President Park Geun-hye.

Kyu-jae's interview of President Park Geun-hye was such a hot issue that as of July 2018, over 2.2 million have watched it.

Since January 2, 2018, Chung Kyu-jae has been running an independent Internet broadcasting program after leaving the Korean Economic Daily.

There is another right-wing journalist whose popularity is on a par with that of Chung Kyu-jae among the right-wing: Cho Gap-je. A former reporter for the monthly magazine Monthly Chosun printed by the Chosun Ilbo, Cho Gap-je has been running his own news media outlet titled Cho Gap-je Dot Com since 2005. As of July 2018, Cho Gap-je TV YouTube channel boasts 135,000 subscribers. Other right-wing journalists who have their own right-wing news websites like Chung Kyu-jae and Cho Gap-je but younger than the two include Hwang Jang-soo and Byun Hee-jae. Hwang Jang-soo is running "Hwang Jang-soo's News Briefing" whose YouTube channel has 165,000 subscribers as of July 2018, and the "Media Watch TV" run by Byun Hee-jae has about 80,000 subscribers. Byun Hee-jae is the author of The Curses of Sohn

Suk-hee that was released in 2017, and he had intensely investigated on suspicions in connection to the JTBC exclusive report that resulted in the impeachment of President Park Geun-hye in the end. On May 24, 2018, the Criminal Investigation Department of Seoul Central District Public Prosecutors' Office requested an arrest warrant for Byun Hee-jae for having damaged the reputation of Sohn Suk-hee, the president of the JTBC news reporting division, when he accused JTBC of having "fabricated stories in their report about the tablet PC." Byun Hee-jae's defense attorney Kang Yong-suk contested that the arrest warrant was unjustified, quoting the "Restraint and Nonrestraint Arrests of Criminals" report found in the "2017 Crime Analysis and Statistics" by the Supreme Prosecutor's Office. Kang claimed that according to the report, the restraining arrest warrant was issued only to 15 out of 17,401 criminals, and that the prosecuting was going after the 0.086% rate of restraining arrest order with regards to Byun's case. But the Seoul Central District Court issued a restraining arrest warrant for Byun Hee-jae on May 29, and Byun is currently detained in the Seoul Detention Center. Does it make sense that a person involved in an active defamation lawsuit is restrained and detained in a cell? Be-

Byun Hee-jae was arrested after pointing out problems of the JTBC report.

sides, Byun Hee-jae is a journalist. The history will tell if the court has made the right decision when it issued the warrant to restrain and detain a journalist Byun Hee-jae for having raised suspicions on another journalist Sohn Suk-hee.

Another notable right-wing online news media is the "Divine Moves," which has 176,000 YouTube subscribers as of July 2018. The Divine Moves was catapulted into fame thanks to the 2017 presidential election. When the Constitutional Court delivered the decision to impeach President Park Geun-hye on March 10, 2017, at 11:00 am, Korea suddenly needed to have a presidential election. The Liberty Korea Party had to rush to pick a presidential candidate, and on March 31, 2017, Hong Jun-pyo was selected as their presidential candidate. By this time, they had just about a month before the election slated on May 9, 2017. Hong Jun-pyo authorized the Divine Moves to have an up-close-and-personal coverage of his campaign activities. This was a tremendous privilege. Shin Hye-sik, the head and host of the Divine Moves, was able to stay close

"The Divine Move" Shin Hye-sik and Hong Jun-pyo, the Liberty Korea Party's presidential candidate.

to the Liberty Korea Party's presidential candidate Hong Jun-pyo, live broadcasting his campaign activities, and delivering Hong's every speech to his right-wing supporters.

YouTube's influence in Korea is continuously growing bigger. According to a report by the Journalists Association dated June 28, 2018, more and more media outlets are uploading their news content on YouTube. In 2013, YTN took quick action when it started uploading their news content on YouTube, and other media outlets such as JTBC and SBS followed the suit. Beginning from 2018, MBC and KBS started uploading their news clips on YouTube as well, according to the report. Those who work in broadcasting companies explain that they are making their news clips available on YouTube to expand the impact of their news content. The Journalists Association report also pointed out that it is inevitable for each broadcasting company to turn to YouTube to meet the demands of the "Z Generation," which refers to those born after 1995 and prefer YouTube over TV.

As seen in this case, the impact of TV and newspapers is expected to grow weaker now that the impact of everybody's must-have device smartphone is continuously growing. Consequently, it is predicted that the power of alternative media will also continue to expand. The Korean press may have been dominated by the KCTU-affiliated NUM for the past 30 years, but with the arrival of the era of smartphone, an opportunity opened its door for the Korean press to break free from the union's influence.

7-4.
MOVING BEYOND THE CONSERVATIVE VS. LIBERAL FRAME

The debates over the terms of conservative and liberal, as well as the left-wing and the right-wing, are not restricted only to Korea. In fact, the debates seem happening throughout the world. In Korea, the term "conservative" has the connotation of "boring and outdated," while the term "liberal" carries the impression of being progressive and future-oriented. This is one of the reasons the young Korean generations are turning away from the conservatives. None of the Korean presidents had lived an uneventful life including the former President Park Geun-hye who was recently impeached and locked up in jail. Perhaps that is the very tragedy of South Korea.

Roh Moo-hyun was another Korean president who had lived a life laden with numerous trials and downfalls. And even in his death, he was exceptional. After he left office, Roh Moo-hyun was interrogated by the prosecution in connection with the accusation that he had received a Piaget watch that cost $200,000 from Park Yeon-cha, the chairman of Taekwang that made sneakers including Nike, and also having him transfer $5 million to his son Roh Geon-ho. Soon after, he leaped to his death from Bueong'i Bawi (lit. Owl's Rock), found in Mt. Bonghwa, Gimhae-si, South Gyeongnam Province on May 23, 2009. After Roh Moo-hyun's suicide, people would connect his death to the death of former Daewoo Construction President Nam Sang-gook, who also jumped from Hannam Bridge to his death after he was implicated to Roh Moo-hyun's impeachment.

Roh Moo-hyun was the first Korean president in our history who had his executive power suspended pending a decision by the Constitutional Court after the National Assembly voted to impeach him for illegal electioneering. On March 12, 2004, the left-leaning Millennium Democratic Party submitted an impeachment motion, and the right-wing Grand National Party and the United Liberal Party agreed to the motion. The National Assembly approved the impeachment with 193 votes in favor of the impeachment and only 2 against it. The impeachment incident all started when Roh voiced support for the Uri Party when he met the press, and his support for a specific political party constituted a violation of Constitutional provisions mandating presents to remain politically impartial. The Millennium Democratic Party was understandably enraged at President Roh, because even though the MDP was credited to making Roh Moo-hyun a president, President Roh voiced his support of the Uri Party which was formed by his supporters who left the Millennium Democratic Party. The United Liberal Democrats was originally a right-leaning political party and objected the impeachment motion that was submitted by the Millennium Democratic Party. But the tables quickly turned around on March 11, 2004, when President Roh Moo-hyun had a special press meeting. In this meeting, President Roh addressed the suspicion that Daewoo Construction President Nam Sang-gook gave $30,000 to Roh Moo-hyun's older brother Roh Geon-pyeong, and openly humiliated Nam by saying, "I hope I will never have to see someone from good school and made a big success comes to visit a man in countryside, bow to him and give money to him." It was a situation where the ROK President humiliated the president of a specific company through a live TV broadcast that was aired to the entire country. On the same day, Nam Sang-gook jumped from Hannam Bridge to his death. After witnessing the whole chain of events that happened on the day, even the United Liberal Democrats changed its position and supported the impeachment motion, and the very next day, the National Assembly voted in favor of the impeachment motion. However, voters started raising question about whether the National Assembly could decide to impeach a rightfully elected president, and this growing negative public opinion contributed to the landslide victory of the Uri Party at the parliament election that happened on April 15, 2004. Then on May 14, 2004 at 11:00am, the Constitutional Court decided to dismiss the impeachment motion. It makes a good contrast to the Court's decision made on March 10, 2017 at 10:00am to impeach President Park Geun-hye.

At any rate, the National Assembly voted to impeach the President, and Roh Moo-hyun's executive power was suspended as of March 12, 2004. He returned to office on May 14 when the Constitution Court decided to dismiss the case. Now, everybody wondered how he would act after he returned to office. His first official activity was a two-hour special speech at Yonsei University on May 27, 2004. In this speech, he made numerous remarks that seemed to carry serious connotations.

"You may speak of all sorts of conservatives — rational conservative, warm conservative, or any other conservative, but at the end of the day,

7. MOVING FORWARD TO THE ERA OF NEW MEDIA

conservatives are all about 'never change'."

"The conservatives are more like 'let the one with power do as he pleases, let the winner take it all, let's be faithful to the survival of the fittest, and law of the jungle is the law of the universe.'"

"In Korea, people often define the conservatives are the Right and the liberals are commies, and that is a cancerous block that interferes progress of the Korean society."

Those remarks clearly showed Roh Moo-hyun's perception of "conservatives." His choice of words was surprising in itself, but it was shocking how confidently he was telling the college students that the conservatives were all about "never change." I was flabbergasted to find that the President of Korea had such a rudimentary dichotomous view of the world and had such a twisted idea about conservatives. If that's the view of the head of the state, imagine what it would be like for the general public. Then I wondered, will it be easy to explain the meaning of conservative in Korea? Or will it be easier to use the term "the Right" instead of "the conservatives"?

When you look at the history of Korea, it might look more appropriate to say the right-wing is progressive and the left-wing is conservative. In Korea, the right-wing is more into free market economy, expansion of cities, and globalism, while the left-wing cares more about the equal distribution of wealth, agricultural community, and nationalism. The construction of Gyeongbu Expressway made a significant contribution to the growth of Korea, because connecting Seoul and Pusan directly translated into the development of the country. Was the right-leaning President Park Chung-hee being conservative when he decided to construct the expressway? Or was he being progressive? And was the left-leaning Kim

Dae-jung, who was a lawmaker at the time, being conservative when he objected the construction of the expressway and advocated balance development of agricultural communities? Or was he being progressive?

Is it still appropriate to apply the meaning of "conservative" that first appeared in the British politics during the 1700s in today's Korea? Even though the terms conservative and progressive are customarily used in the United States, that doesn't mean the same terms should be applied in Korea as well. Nevertheless, the Korean press are using the right-wing for conservatives and the left-wing for progressives in their reports. The leftists hate to be defined as "leftists." As President Roh Moo-hyun pointed out to the Yonsei students on May 27, 2004, they think the term "the left" is synonymous with "commies." It makes me feel that the President Roh Moo-hyun was instructing them not to use the terms of the left and the right and use the terms of conservatives and progressives instead.

The right and the left are terms that have no value judgments, but the conservative and the progressive are terms that have value judgements. However, the leftists in Korea claim the Left is a term used for commies and refuse to be defined as "leftist." The Korean press is faithfully following the leftists' claim and use only the conservative and the progressive, and do not use the terms of the left and the right. But the press is showing double standards because they use the terms of the left-wing and the right-wing when they refer to foreign governments. And reporters also use the term of "extreme right-wing group" when they try to belittle right-wing citizen groups. Then why the journalists are not using the term of "extreme left-wing group" at all? That shows how double-faced the Korean journalists really are.

During the presidential election in 2017, the presidential candidate Hong Jun-pyo used the terms of "the right-wing" and "the left-wing" instead of "the conservatives" and "the progressive". After the presidential election was over, Hong Jun-pyo became the leader of the Liberty Korea Party, and appeared in a variety program. While appearing in the program called "Pot Stand" that was aired on July 25, 2017, Hong Jun-pyo told the host Lee Kyung-gyu:

"I have long since preferred to distinguish people as right and left rather than conservative and progressive."
"It may sound like the conservative is a relic left by antiquated political group, but progressive is a word that appeals to young people."
"We have to get it straight and realize the right-wing cares freedom as the core value, while the left-wing cares about equality as the core value."

He is right a hundred percent. But the press refuses to let go of their practice of distinguishing people either as conservative or progressive. Even the leading right-wing media outlets such as Chosun Ilbo are insisting on distinguishing people as conservative or progressive. This is a problem we have to resolve. I think Chosun Ilbo is just being stubborn with regards to the terms, and I think it is slightly different from other left-leaning media outlets. According to the book *War of Terms* (2016), co-authored by Hyun Jin-kwon and Kim In-young, "progressive" is a word that means "moving forward," while the "conservative" is a word that means "remaining." Therefore, the conservative is in a disadvantageous position beginning from the start. And the progressive is one level above the conservative because it has the connotation that satisfy the human instinct that pursues positive value, growth, and improvement. Therefore, the conservatives must be described as the "right-wing" and the progressive, the "left-wing" in the press. But can this change happen in the Korean press easily? There is only one solution: The right-wing political parties must take the lead in refusing to be defined as "conservatives." Recently, Korean rightist political parties are using the term "conservative right-wing." It's truly ridiculous. They are using the term "right-wing" but is adding the term "conservative" to it. Does that mean the right-wing camp is admitting that they are not progressive? If they are determined to use the term "right-wing," they must let go of the term "conservative." And they also have to define themselves as "progressive right-wing." That's is what the Name Rectification Campaign is all about. If the right-wing political parties don't take the lead in this name rectification campaign, they will permanently fall behind the left-wing political parties in the race.

8. EPILOGUE

The 1987 "June Uprising" that was triggered by the death of Park Jong-chul was a big turning point in Korea. Park Jong-chul was a PD ideologist who followed Marxism-Leninism and advocated class struggle, but his death effectuated the shift of hegemony of student movements in Korea from PD to NL, which has connection to the North's *Juche* Ideology.

Surely PD lie also dream of the Soviet-style communist revolution. But NL's connection to the North matters more to the student movements because NL cares more about the union of the South and the North as one nation than the class struggle.

More than anything, NL boasts more threatening impact because, unlike PD, NL willingly accept populism and popularism.

Those who had participated in the 1987 "June Uprising" moved up the ladders in the Korean society in various fields and contributed to charting the future of Korea.

These people are called the "386 Generation." The word first appeared in around 1997, and it means those who were born in the 1960s, went to college in the 1980s, and now are in their 50s.

NL doesn't distinguish Korea into the South and the North, and it cares about the South and the North being one nation. Therefore, their main claims are anti-Americanism and unification. Within NL, there are a group of ideologists called *Jusapa*, who are following the Juche ideology complied by Kim Jong-il, the father of the current leader of the North Kim Jong-un. This is a fact that indicates how close the *Jusapa* ideologists are with the North.

It was just a few years ago on December 19, 2014 that our Constitutional Court made a decision to disband the Unified Progressive Party, majority of whose lawmaker members are the NL ideologists. Lawmaker Lee Seok-ki who was a member of the Unified Progressive Party, was found to have instructed his subordinates to "be ready to raid communication, oil storage facilities, and railroads" because "the day of revolution is coming."

The anti-American movement started in full swing after NL became the center of student movements in the wake of the 1987 June Uprising. In 1989, an NL activist group named "Anti-American Death-defying National Salvation Corps," which was affiliated with the National Council of Student Representatives, raided and took over the official residence of the US Ambassador to Korea and detonated homemade bombs.

The problem is that such a violent group of NL student activists took over majority of important government posts with the inception of the left-wing Kim Dae-jung administration in 1997. And they also became journalists working in different media outlets and faithfully carried out their mission. It was during the Kim Dae-jung administration that the anti-American sentiment reached its peak in Korea.

The Korean press poured oil on the growing anti-American sentiment by continuously reporting coverages on the so-called No Gun Ri Incident, which was about the US soldiers having shelled and killed numerous Korean civilians during the Korean War.

A citizen group called the Green Korea fanned the anti-American sentiment by claiming that USFK secretly released a toxic chemical known as formaldehyde into the Han River.

And the director Bong Joon-ho released a movie "Host" with a scene that accused USFK.

The US national short track skater Ohno became the public enemy to Koreans during the 2002 Salt Lake Winter Olympics, and Korean's rage against Ohno added more fuel to the anti-American sentiment.

But when two Korean schoolgirls Shim Mi-seon and Shin Hyo-soon were hit by an armored US vehicle and crushed to death on June 13, 2002. This incident was soon followed by large-scale candlelight rallies where Koreans protested and criticized Americans.

Just a few days later on June 29, the North Korean soldiers opened fire and killed six South Korean navy, but their deaths were largely ignored. The very next day, President Kim Dae-jung left for Yokohama, Japan, to watch the World Cup final between Brazil and Germany.

In 2008, Korea witnessed another round of candlelight rallies, and this time they were protesting against the US beef imports. People casually spread such terrifying rumors that if you eat the US beef imports, you will catch the "human mad cow disease" and die after having your brains perforated. Reports by the Korea's second largest broadcasting company MBC greatly contributed to the spread of such nonsense rumors. Today, however, Koreans love the US beef imports, and nobody has died after eating the US beef and having their brains perforated.

Now, after Moon Jae-in became the President, the many of the former NL student activists became important government officials. The former NL student activists are also working not just in government agencies, but also in media outlets, courts, lawyer groups, and educational institutions. Today's Korean press is ruled by the KCTU-affiliated NUM. The majority of KCTU members also belong to the NL. The employees of Naver, the portal site that boasts the biggest influence in Korea, are also joining the KCTU. That means the main power of Korea is in the hand of the KCTU, a union where NL has a big influence. And the essence of the NL ideology is anti-American and two Korea being one nation.

The Korean press is shamelessly praising the North's Kim Jong-un regime and ignoring the human rights violations against North Koreans.

In June of 2018, Hankook Ilbo, one of the major media outlets in Korea, had the audacity to print an in article that claimed, "Peace on the Korean peninsula is more important than human rights in North Korea." In April 2018, MBC reported that "Seven out of ten Koreans trust Kim Jong-un."

As if praising the murderous dictator Kim Jong-un is not enough, the Korean Press praised Kim Jong-un's sister, Kim Yo-jong, introducing her as a member of the "Mount Baekdu Bloodline" in their headlines. These news outlets printed and broadcasted one after another reports whose level made us wonder if we are back to the era of monarchy in this 21st century.

When the US Army tried to deploy THAAD on the Korean Peninsula, numerous media outlets reported that the radar from THAAD would cause people to get harmed by its electromagnetic waves, and leftist lawmakers spread ungrounded rumor that the electromagnetic wave coming from the THAAD radar would fry up human bodies.

On February 9, 2018, the US Vice President Mike Pence came to visit Korea for the Pyeongchang Winter Olympics and asked Korean officials not to make him cross paths with the North's delegate Kim Young-nam, but President Moon ignored Pence's request, and made him sit on the same table with Kim Young-nam. When Pence left the venue five minutes later, the Korean press blamed Vice President Pence, and claimed he had made diplomatic discourtesy.

Now, the Korean press has to move beyond the current of NL, which naturally leads to anti-America, pro-North ideology. However, a new media environment seems to hold the key to naturally solve this problem. Korea being an acclaimed IT superpower, practically all Koreans beginning from elementary students to the seniors in their 80s have their own smart phone. Therefore, there is almost nobody who doesn't enjoy watching videos on YouTube. It is rather hard to find people who sit and watch news on TV at certain time or buy and read printed newspapers. That means we are entering an era where the Korean press that is currently dominated by KCTU-affiliated NUM cannot unleash its influence.

As we stand at the cusp of a new era when new media content becomes more important than ever, new alternative media that is free from the influence of NL should flourish. NL that advocates anti-America pro-North ideology will surely channel all its resources into alternative media such as YouTube. For that reason, the right-wing camp is called on to rush and focus their efforts in the development of content that is suitable for alternative media.

9. WORKS CITED

- Byun Hee-jae. *The Curses of Sohn Suk-hee*. Media Silk, 2017.
- Cho, Hyung-gon. *The Sophistry of Minbyun*. Baeknyundongan, 2014.
- Choi, Do-young, and Kang-won Kim. *What Media Has Done Under 10 Years of Leftist Government*. Bibong Publishing, 2013.
- David Straub. *Anti-Americanism in Democratizing South Korea*. Sanchurum, 2017.
- Hong, Ji-soo. *The Political Correctness That Brought Victory to Trump*. Book and People, 2017.
- Lee, Myung-joon. *How they become Jusapa*. Bao, 2012.
- Nah, Eun-young. *Media Psychology*. Hannarae, 2016.
- Nam, Jeong-wook. *Goodbye 386*. Book and People, 2014.
- New Media Forum. Field Records, *Media Labor Union's 20 Years of Pro-democracy Movement*. Communication Books, 2014.
- Park, Chan-soo. *Modern History of NL*. Inmool gwa Sasang, 2017.
- Shim, Yang-seop. Analyzing Anti-Americanism. Edam Books, 2010.
- Sung, Chang-kyung. *Crazy Media*. Nanum, 2018.